| DATE | | | |
|------|------|------|------|
| SEP 1 0 1981 | | | |
| OCT 2 1981 | | | |
| NOV 9 1981 | | | |
| FEB 5 1982 | | | |
| APR 2 2 1982 | | | |
| MAY 2 1 1982 | | | |
| JUN 5 1982 | | | |
| JY 1 '83 | | | |
| AUG 2 0 1983 | | | |
| AUG 2 7 1996 | | | |
| AUG 6 1997 | | | |
| | | | |
| MAR 0 1 1999 | | | |

# At Home On

# St. Simons

Eugenia Price

PEACHTREE PUBLISHERS LIMITED

Published by
PEACHTREE PUBLISHERS, LTD.
494 Armour Circle, N. E.
Atlanta, Georgia 30324

Copyright © 1981   Eugenia Price, Text
Critt Graham, Illustrations

Manufactured in the United States of America

Book and cover design by Critt Graham

First Edition

ISBN: 0-931948-16-9
Library of Congress Catalog Card Number 81-1412

*For Carol and the late Larry Case, who first published these columns, and for my mother, who bothered to save them.*

# Contents

To Be Read First 1

Coming Home 10

Silence 12

Mr. Winn Still Blooms 20

Dear Mary 24

Bird Notes 28

A Day of Rest 37

Try Looking in the Rain 43

The Light at Christmas 47

Wonder and Sacrilege 51

No Pat Answers 55

I Am a Baseball Nut 59

An Unforgettable Man 64

A Very Special Book 69

Love Came Down 75

Journey to Reality 80

Only Customs Have Changed 83

We Are Blessed 88

# To Be Read First

I am writing these lines at the beginning of a new decade—the decade of the 1980s—after having lived almost twenty years on St. Simons Island, Georgia. They are certainly not the first lines I've written about the lush, sheltering, buggy, enchanted cosmos that is this particular coastal island. Over the past years there have been three novels laid here, plus *St. Simons Memoir* and *Diary of a Novel*. In all these, as historical fiction and autobiography, I have attempted to delineate the essence of this once wild little island cosmos.

My dictionary declares that "cosmos" means "the universe conceived as an orderly, harmonious system." St. Simons a universe? Orderly? Harmonious? Its nature, yes. Season follows season in nature's orderly fashion. Cardinals mate with other cardinals; azalea bushes sprout azalea buds, wisteria vines wisteria buds; French mulberries and star-flowers appear on schedule. Still, where people live, they intervene to change natural order and harmony; and people have been *busy* on my island. "Order" seems to be missing entirely from our development, and at least the old "harmony" among islanders has lessened. It is no longer safe to leave doors unlocked or to walk alone on the beach. "Harmonious" certainly does not describe the performance of the local government. More trees are falling, the woods are being hacked and bulldozed away. And yet I stick with that word "cosmos."

Distinct from the other barrier islands off the coast of Georgia, St. Simons is, in its own way, a small, unique universe, harmonious and orderly at its core—its soul—in spite of external disorder and rampant growth; different, in a way no one has yet managed to explain. And perhaps this

1

very difference springs from the fact that its history *is* singular. You see, unlike the other islands, St. Simons has never been privately owned. That is, except for God, who thought it up in the first place, no one owner has ever legally been in possession of St. Simons Island. In a sense, I suppose one could say that the colonial government of Georgia owned it back in the 1700s, but even then its population was as varied and individual as now. No one family has ever cared for, planted, or guarded it. Even in his day, the Spaniards gave General Oglethorpe a hard time protecting it. Then at a later period, roughly twelve plantation families owned the little strip of land.

And now look! I am told that more than twelve hundred houses will be built soon in the vicinity of Christ Church on the as yet unspoiled end of the island at Frederica, close by the fort. There aren't enough of us in this section now to get cable TV. How much change will twelve hundred new buildings cause? How much disorder? How much disharmony?

Perhaps not too much, really. And my ability to write that proves to me, at least, that the *un*changing, harmonious, orderly cosmic heart of this island has at last penetrated *me*. Once the mere thought of the destruction of these "dear, dark woods" made me physically ill. Oh, the beauty as we all know it now, around Christ Church and Fort Frederica, will be drastically changed. Frederica will look much like any other subdivision. There is talk of St. Simons being incorporated so that we will no longer be a helpless, rather affluent appendage of the sprawling Glynn County government. On the other hand, there is talk of consolidation with the remainder of the county, which, of course, would make us an instant city—I presume called Brunswick. Change and the threats of change buffet us daily.

2

But can such radical changes really wipe out the *inner* essence of the unique little cosmos that for years has attracted even United States presidents in need of shelter and peace and rest and a restored sense of wonder?

When Joyce Blackburn and I first discovered this light-struck, tree-and-vine-choked small cosmos back in 1961, St. Simons was simple and quiet and lovely and slow—affluent only in its singular beauty. Islanders were mainly warm-hearted, easy-living folk. *Less* than 3,000 strong. Each a strong individualist, in his or her own way; each an Islander. I see us beginning to blur together now. There are four times as many Islanders, and our "master plan" anticipates 20,000 more!

Do I deplore this? Yes, for obvious reasons. And yet I don't altogether deplore it, because each new person who makes the final drive across the marshes and salt creeks to live on St. Simons "forever," as we did, seems as much in love with it and as full of joy to be here as were we all those years ago. For these growing numbers of newcomers, the old magic holds. The cosmos remains. They are *on* St. Simons—at last—to stay. I confess at times to marveling at their joy and gladness, because the Island is so changed for me. And yet, and yet, even the ongoing debate about a second causeway and the four-laning of Frederica and Demere roads in no way seems to dim the newcomer's elevation of spirit at having "come home" at last.

"Four-lane Frederica Road?" a new resident gasped when I mentioned it to her in the grocery store the other day. Her face pale, she reeled a little, and then that determined smile returned, as her color returned. "Well, it's still St. Simons Island, and I don't want to be any other place on the face of this old earth!"

Nor do I.

Of course a new causeway, or four-laning the present one over a ghastly, high, view-distorting set of bridges, is supposed to make it safe for Islanders when hurricanes and tidal waves come. Well, I no longer fear the Island's geography, and, except for moments of stabbing memory, I have stopped being afraid for St. Simons. I loathe what is happening; but you see, some mystical part of the Island's core has entered mine. For a time, I considered calling this book *Inner Island*. Living here for twenty years has helped me find an inner island of my own. A quiet, inner refuge where, some of the time at least, God and I attempt to keep me grateful and accepting. I have stopped fighting. Today, from my office window, I can still see only live oaks and breeze-stirred moss and pine trees and lush sweet gum leaves. If I walk to my bedroom window, I can still see the small back marsh, where spider webs go on glistening at dawn and out of which a full moon continues to rise.

Servicemen still come promptly when appliances break down, and the people at Georgia Power and Southern Bell are still kind and sympathetic when we call to report trouble. Our storekeeper friends seldom lose their smiles when my readers go on trying to find out where I live; and Sarah Edmond and Monroe Wilson are friends and not just employees who come to clean our house and mow our lawn. A meal at Alphonza Ramsey's Plantation Club, at Blanche's Courtyard, or at Gantt's is as warm and welcoming an experience as a meal on Lorah Plemmons's back porch once was. This may all change when those terrifying population projections are at last fact. But I choose to believe not.

My period of rebellion at what "they're doing" to St. Simons seems, at least most of the time, to have passed. The

4

heart of the once wild, nearly primitive little cosmos remains: the enduring essence, which I pray has really become a part of me.

Day follows day and St. Simons goes on, unprotected by single ownership or even by state or federal ownership as with the other barrier islands. Perhaps it garners inner strength from this very fate of having fallen into the hands of lots and lots of people, some of whom still seem intent upon grabbing more and more money from it for themselves.

I've been accused of that, and I understand the accusation. God knows that when I wrote *The Beloved Invader*, my first novel laid here, I had no earthly reason to believe that it would sell as it did and bring people flocking to Christ Church at Frederica, books in hand, to search out the graves of my main characters who lie buried there. The Chamber of Commerce honored me for having done this—others resent me. Some days I resent myself. I resented myself to the extent that as soon as the St. Simons trilogy was written and my contracts fulfilled, I moved the locale of my next novels to St. Augustine, Florida. And for the next one, I will change locales again—to Savannah.

Yet, if my mail is any indication and if my own heart's desire counts, St. Simons will remain, to my readers and to me, a special place to be. My *home*. Part of the reason that is true is because in a particular way, the Island is, *in itself*, harmonious, orderly. A cosmos. With a life of its own. Novelists, perhaps, tend to anthropomorphize places and things. I even name my cars. It is, then, no surprise that I tend to give St. Simons a life of its own, a personality, a heart, a will to survive, in spite of high bridges and four-laned roads and bulldozers. There are times when I speak aloud to it: "You really are trying to *remain yourself*, aren't you, Island?"

And then I notice new, determined bright green vines struggling to cover the stump of a fallen tree, and I cheer.

The Indians called the St. Johns River, which flows north instead of south, We-la-ka: "The river with a way of its own." No one will ever shake my steadfast belief that St. Simons has a sheltering, seductive, singular, strong "way of its own."

At first I took for granted that everyone loved the Island for the same reasons I loved it—long-needled pines that catch the ever-changing light; resurrection ferns burgeoning along wide-branched oaks after a heavy rain; gold, gold leaves of twining bullis grapevines in autumn. I assumed everyone loved the Island history, its plantation families, its attraction not only to the military mind of General James Edward Oglethorpe, Georgia's founder, but to his heart as well. This is not necessarily true. These attractions, so fascinating to me, do not draw everyone who loves St. Simons. Even my dear friends, the oldtimers, didn't seem to know a lot about Island history. Few brightened with anything resembling proud recognition when Oglethorpe's name was mentioned. Many had never noticed the wonder of resurrection ferns, "risen from the dead" after a good rain. They all loved Island grapes, but few had thought about the (to me) exciting fact that God decorates His own trees at Christmas with those bright strands of yellow-leafed vines. No matter. *They loved the Island,* and their love was contagious.

New residents and visitors come for reasons which would certainly not attract me. Retirement, to rear their children here, golf, tennis, the beach, fishing. I have no children, never mean to retire, don't fish or play golf or tennis, much prefer James Gould's old plantation site as it once was: a breathtaking stand of tall trees and vines and palmetto. But St. Simons *is* a cosmos. With magnets enough for us all. It is

6

a many-faceted place, its very nature reaching as wide as the few remaining giant oaks to embrace all kinds of folk, giving of itself, its ocean, its sky, its awesome Island light—according to our needs.

In spite of the changes which were just beginning during the years in which I wrote most of what you will read in this book, St. Simons is still giving. And, to me at least, that is proof that there is in its light-shot, winter-gray, summer-steaming, wild, gentle heart, a singular balm for everyone. People come here to find solace from grief, to find a simpler way of life, to slow down, to work, to play, to study, to paint, to write books. To be. To find inner harmony, inner order. A safe personal cosmos. Home—for always, or for a week.

Oh, I confess to a period of wondering, shortly after I finished writing the St. Simons trilogy of novels, if I had fallen as deeply in love with the Island as I thought. My research was over, the books published. My writer's energies, heart, and mind were suddenly deep in the lives of the people and the history of quaint, altogether charming St. Augustine. The onslaught of development had truly begun on St. Simons Island, and now and then, driving alone to Florida for research, I'd ask myself: "Wasn't it really just the fact that there, for the first time in your entire life, you found the kind of *writing* you most love? The Island gave you that. Do you really love St. Simons *itself* the way you once did?"

For a time, I wasn't sure. My answer has now become clear. *I have come home.* This is my place to be. Even without my old and beloved friends mentioned in this book—Lorah Plemmons, Mary and Dutch Everett, Berta and Douglas Taylor, the N.C. Youngs. They are all gone. A heart-breaking number of great trees are gone, too. But the Island is still here and I still belong to it. Undoubtedly I handle some of

7

the drastic outward changes by escaping into my novelist's imagination. When I drive down Frederica Road now, I don't look at what is actually there. I "see" it as I wrote of it, and the peace holds. Even though so much is gone. So many trees, acres of bright-dark woods. So many friends. In fact, the laughing young man who talked me into writing these columns which you are about to read is gone from the Island he loved with all his generous, creative heart. This little book would not exist had not the late Larry Case and his Carol urged me to write "about anything that interests you" for *Coastal Illustrated*, which they founded back in the late 1960s. I have dedicated *At Home on St. Simons* to them, with love and gratitude. Carol is still here—strong, busy and bright of spirit, even without Larry. I wondered, frankly, if she could bear to stay. They were so much a part of life on St. Simons—together. More proof, I suppose, that the healing balm is here for anyone willing to enter in.

I have also dedicated *At Home on St. Simons* to my mother, Anna S. Price, who, remarkably for a mother living in another part of the country, has from the begining accepted and rejoiced in the fact that her only daughter found "home" when she found St. Simons Island. With Larry and Carol, Mother shares responsibility for the very existence of this book. She is not a saver by nature, but she did save all my *Coastal Illustrated* columns, made the initial selections and, as always, encouraged me to put them between covers. Mother is no longer able to travel to the Island, but in a very real way, as she did so often in the period about which you will now read, she can "visit" me still because she remembers it as it once was.

To Gene-Gabriel Moore, of Public Broadcasting's *By-line*, I owe the whole idea for having done *At Home on St.*

8

*Simons*. To Joyce Blackburn, who found St. Simons with me, I owe and owe and owe.

Quite simply, this is a selected group of musings, entirely at random, from earlier days on the Island which has indeed become my *home*.

# CHAPTER I

## *Coming Home*

Late in 1961, Joyce Blackburn and I were traveling down the East Coast toward the next scheduled autographing party for my then current book, *Beloved World*, when we discovered a two-day leeway in our itinerary. We made the discovery on the outskirts of Charleston, South Carolina, got out a roadmap, and, because we liked the sound of its name, picked St. Simons Island, Georgia, as a place to rest for those two days. The AAA guidebook told us that the Wesleys had preached on St. Simons in Oglethorpe's time; that Aaron Burr had hidden out at a plantation on the north end of St. Simons; and that in memory of his young bride who had died on their honeymoon, Rev. Anson Greene Phelps Dodge, Jr., had rebuilt Christ Church Frederica.

"Let's go there," I said. "I'm fascinated with this man Anson Dodge even more than with the Wesleys and Aaron Burr and Oglethorpe!"

By noon of our first day on St. Simons, I knew I had to

write a novel about the Reverend Mr. Dodge. I had been hunting during my then extensive travels for a story based on truth which would make a biographical novel. *The Beloved Invader* was published in 1965, the very month Joyce Blackburn and I moved to St. Simons to stay, I hope, forever. Long before we found the piece of land we wanted on which to build our home, we owned a small plot in Christ Church churchyard. "Even if we wind up selling the plot at least I can say that for a little while I owned a piece of St. Simons!"

We found St. Simons the day after Thanksgiving, and this will always be an anniversary for us both. From our first glimpse by that special brown-gold autumn light, we were in love with it. We had arrived after dark, and the moss hanging from the shadowy trees, the air rank with the acrid smell of industry in Brunswick, had not been what one would call inviting. But the next morning, the sun took care of all that, and from that special Friday in November 1961 to now, our hearts have lived in coastal Georgia.

For twelve long years of traveling, from one speaking engagement to another, the length and breadth of this land, I had consciously looked for the one place where I felt I belonged. Knowing that someday I would stop all that traveling and leave the crowded city, I searched and searched in every state of the union. Until I found St. Simons Island, I had almost settled on the Big Sur country in northern California. When I saw coastal Georgia—most especially the Frederica section of St. Simons—all doubts were gone. I had come home to stay.

11

# CHAPTER II

# *Silence*

J ust as dawn began to slip over the small marsh behind my house on a chilly January morning, I opened my garage doors to what represented a near miracle to these once city-deafened ears. I saw nothing but the first sky full of roseate light—pale blue around the edges—as the new wonder broke out of the ocean to the east and hung above the thick miasma still tucked snugly at the marsh margins, but what I heard I will never forget. I was in a hurry to catch the morning flight to Atlanta, but even if I had missed that plane, I would have stopped long enough to listen to the sudden sounds moving swiftly across the misty marsh that special dawn. All sorts of wrong, city-ignorant thoughts flashed through my mind as I stood there. Alligators? Dog over from Harrington hunting in the marshes? No. The sounds were too thin for dogs, and there are no alligators in my marsh anymore. Then I knew what it was I was hearing. Soft, rapid hoofbeats on the black marsh mud, scarcely rustling the dew-drenched spartina grasses, thudding, flying away from

me, their beat diminishing, fading, but held to my ears by the unbelievable quiet of a marsh morning—until, unmistakably, one, then two, then three deer, invisible in the mist, splashed into the waters of Dunbar Creek and began to swim steadily to the other side.

I had frightened them, opening my old-fashioned, quite noisy garage doors so suddenly at a time of day no sound disturbs them from my house on its lonely point of land. And even in their flight, they had blessed me. They had given me a set-apart moment of the kind of delight one person can never give to another person. A silence accentuated by their flying hooves and their quick swim across the salt creek—silence I will never forget.

Sudden human actions don't accentuate silence as wild things do. We clutter silence with too much talk, too much crying out when we are afraid. I had only a moment to listen that morning, but I have kept the moment and I am still learning from it.

The deer are almost gone from St. Simons Island. My three invisible marsh travelers would not have been there if the marsh had not been there, if it had been filled and built on and dead forever.

Man needs silence. It is so rare a thing now to find a part of one minute in which we can still "hear" the silence—even on St. Simons Island. I live in a remote place, and in one of those infrequent times when there is not even one plane in the air, not one power saw mutilating a single tree, I stop typing, stop reading, stop whatever I'm doing to listen. It happens so seldom anymore.

The marshes across which my three dawn visitors fled help hold what silence we still possess in coastal Georgia.

I was on my way that morning to Atlanta in order to testify

before a Senate hearing for all of us who still care, on behalf of what might be our last chance to save our beloved marshlands: Georgia state Rep. Reid Harris's Wetlands Protection bill. It seems very strange to most of us that anyone would fight a measure like this, but they are fighting it. Otherwise kind, good people are fighting it.

As I stood listening to the miracle of the deer beside my own little stretch of mist-covered marsh that morning, I was glad I had decided to put off my work and go. Glad and grateful that I could go. One or two other Islanders went too. Many people sent letters and telegrams. Maybe we helped a little.

*       *       *

Before beginning to write today, I sat at my desk for fifteen minutes, my doors open to the upstairs porch, listening, still thinking of silence. For exactly twelve seconds of that fifteen minutes, there was no grinding plane motor of any description overhead! This has to be some kind of record. I have tried this before in the years I have lived on St. Simons Island, desperately needing to identify with the Island in the old days before man made his first rackety flying machine. People have been kind enough to say I write rather realistically of the long-gone silences, the sound of bird songs, and the clatter of the marsh hens with only the wind around them. I wonder about this. My little five-to-twelve-second intervals of no roaring in the sky could not possible give me "research" time on silence, the kind of silence men and women knew in our beloved Golden Isles even as recently as the turn of the century. If I write "silence" realistically, it must be because I

15

am a novelist and not a reporter. I seldom experience it.

Almost no one experiences silence anymore anywhere on the face of the earth. In the West perhaps. I do remember periods of genuine silence in the mountains of Wyoming, on the Mojave Desert. But even there they are broken eventually by a cross-country jet plane, out of sight perhaps, but roaring.

Silence is so rare on St. Simons Island that even in the woods where I live, where no automobile can drive by, when the rare moments come, they are arresting. We would be better people, more aware of one another's needs, if it were possible for us to experience silence just once in a while.

People who manufacture or fly these buzzing little jobs that fill our once-quiet sky will hate me, of course. Will consider me eccentric. I suppose I am, but I am simply overcome now and then with hunger for silence. For silence and time enough to think again—deeply, not off the top of my head between things. Between planes zooming across the sky, cars speeding down our roads; between telephone calls and determined, helmeted people on motorcycles; through the agonized scream of another power saw destroying another tree. (Now and then I'm sure it's the tree that's screaming, not the saw.)

No one told me I was buying land in the flight-path of Glynco Naval Air Station. I suppose I would have been philosophical about it if I had known. I'm as inconsistent as everyone else. I wanted this piece of land—no other. I'm sure I would have bought it regardless. But I doubt that it is all Glynco which causes my longing for silence. True, a plane once jettisoned two bright orange fuel tanks just a stone's throw from the roof of my house. The deafening explosion set the marsh afire, and two helicopters from Glynco

16

shattered the silence, as only helicopters can do, for almost two hours trying to put out the fire in the marsh and pry out the half-buried gas tanks. Of course, I could have been killed. So could my yard man, who tried to hide behind a big oak tree when the screaming "bombs" scattered the birds and shook my house to its foundations.

At Glynco they told me in very polite "public relations" voices that it wasn't one of their planes. It was a jet from God knows where, trying to land at Jacksonville, suddenly becoming bored or overburdened with two fuel-filled tanks, deciding to get rid of them over the ocean missing it only by six miles or so—missing my house by a few hundred feet.

I think maybe only about half of the thunder is from whatever they do at Glynco. The rest is from private citizens hurrying to get wherever they're going, afraid of the silence. Afraid of staying one place long enough to miss making that extra big deal, afraid to miss a round of golf or the glorious opportunity to fire a rifle-blast into the head of an island deer or a marsh hen. Afraid to stop long enough to think. To be alone. Needing to get there. Needing to "hurry up" in order to relax on a beach. "If I hurry—if I buy a plane and fly—I can have a speedy time of rest and relaxation." Aren't we peculiar? And contradictory? And pathetic?

This is not a treatise designed to put down planes or the people who fly them. Some of my best friends fly planes. It is just a small period of musing about how little we think of the other fellow, how lost we are without motors roaring. I'm sure there is a special kind of exhilaration in owning one's own plane, in taking off into the once "wild blue yonder." There must be a genuinely freeing moment of feeling one is leaving earth and all its problems behind. Just a moment, of course, because one is there so soon, back on the troubled

17

earth again. No thought, I'm sure, about what the cherished little plane is doing to nerve-endings on the earth below.

I didn't think of any of this as long as I lived in Chicago. There was so much noise there, so constantly, I was seldom aware of hearing a plane.

St. Simons Island, all of the Golden Isles, are deceptive. One expects it to be different here, and really it was, even in 1960. I remember standing one evening in 1961 on the winding road to the old Island dump, the only one left which looked anything like the roads I was trying to describe in *The Beloved Invader.* For one minute and five seconds, I stood in that narrow, tree-lined sandy road and heard only a cardinal, one wren shouting, and a squirrel barking in the woods behind me. I will never forget that tiny fragment of time.

(I tried "listening" again just now. By my watch, there were seven seconds without a plane overhead. I'm thankful.)

Of course, there is not one thing anyone can or will do about our loss of silence. I hope we will one day see our big industries beginning to do more than talk about their splendid, expensive future plans to stop contaminating our air and our rivers. (Something pouring black smoke into the air from the mainland blocks the view of the sunset from my house every now and then.)

But I doubt that anything can or will ever be done about noise. Those of us who are blessed enough to be living away from metropolitan centers must double our efforts to learn inner balance. Above all, we must not stop being expectant. If I ever grow so callous as not to listen and hope for a moment's real silence, I will hate myself. I will bore myself as do the poor people who have to have noise.

What can we do, those few fringe people among us who still long for quiet and time to think? What can we do? Make

18

the most of the times we are fortunate enough to find. Half a minute—twelve seconds—these are terribly important. Silence holds a quality of life which leaps the limitations of the ticking of our clocks. Eternity will prove this to us, difficult as it is for us to comprehend now.

I learn about God in the silence. Without even trying to concentrate on Him, I find I have experienced a certainty during those five or seven seconds that strengthens my inner self.

These days, I have written month after month about the people who lived on St. Simons Island in the year 1807. This is quite a trick. Our lives are almost totally reversed. The Goulds of New St. Clair and Black Banks wrote of their longing to have something to break the monotony. On St. Simons Island at Frederica now, I long for just one full minute unfractured by a motor of any kind.

We are peculiar people, meant, I believe, to draw strength from a "still small voice." Our hope is to learn somehow to keep the quiet inside. To refuse invasion. No to refuse responsibility. Not to refuse people who matter or who need us. But to refuse to waste our own inner quiet, even as the little waspy private planes puncture our efforts, even as the gasoline tanks explode near our houses and as the monster trucks roar by. If we try, if we really concentrate on the values no noise can demolish, we might—oh, we might even reach the place of inner awareness where we will be able to live above the shriek of the power saw and the racket of the helmeted, determined people on motorcycles.

I just tried again. This time seventeen seconds! I am rested inside by it, ready to start writing for the day.

19

# CHAPTER III

# Mr. Winn Still Blooms

In the short, still sequestered, still wild and lovely stretch of Frederica Road from the First African Baptist Church to Christ Church, one can still "feel" the old Island, still try to imagine what it must have been like "then." Many of my friends, fortunate enough to have lived all or most of their lives here, tell me that the continuing loss of the tangles of smilax, honeysuckle, oaks, palmetto, bindweed, and little pine and sweet gum thickets which once made a shadowy, sun-streaked "cozy" of Frederica Road, hurts them more than it hurts those of us who found the wonder after it had begun to give way to "progress."

Well, I don't know. Is it worse to have loved and lost than not to have loved at all? I have written about "old St. Simons" and readers are kind enough to visit us now, their books under their arms, trying, along with the author, to imagine how it must have been. Good readers must have imaginations, too.

At any rate, some spring—late in April or early in

May—drive up Frederica Road all the way to Christ Church. Once you reach Harrington, the Island begins to look like the storybook Island visitors envision, if my mail is any indication. The little heart-shaped leaves of our wild grapevines still tangle haphazardly up and down the gums and oaks and pines. Harrington residents love their trees. They are still there forming twisted, giant arbors for the random vines once so a part of St. Simons. Just north of the African Baptist Church there is one spot where the wide spreading oak branches of a few old monarchs arch almost across the road, as they once did for nearly the entire length of our one north-south road.

Resurrection ferns, after a good, soaking rain, adorn their branches, and when fall comes, the wild grapevines, as yellow as butter, race up and down and across and around the old trees.

But in the spring, be on the lookout for what I call the "Mr. Winn riot." The Rev. Mr. David Watson Winn, Anson Dodge's choice to succeed him as rector of Christ Church Frederica, certainly was one of the cheeriest, most loved, and most valued men ever to live on St. Simons. Christ Church, during the plantation days the only Island church, is still our most romantic, most naturally beautiful spot. The men who have preached there have all made their separate contributions to the colorful past of this little sandy strip of land— even old Bosomworth, whose contribution was not exactly of a holy nature. Of course, I have written at length about the work of the Rev. Anson Greene Phelps Dodge, Jr., the "beloved invader" from the North, who built the present, elegantly simply little church.

But this is a column about his successor, Watson Winn, whose laughter and good humor I sometimes imagine I

21

knew, too. The man was loved by everyone, so far as I can discover, and I love him too, if only for the "Mr. Winn riot" which bursts faithfully into color each spring along the roadsides at the north end of the Island.

Before beginning this, I called one of the dearest people on earth to me, Mrs. Lorah Plemmons, who lives in her white cottage back in the woods at Frederica and who blesses our lives, not only with her fantastic memory concerning the old days on St. Simons, but with her altogether contemporary spirit and humor. I called her to be sure I'd remembered her story about the "Mr. Winn riot" correctly. You see, the riot he caused is a riot of color—bright, cheering orange-colored blossoms which burst upon us from rather fragile looking bushes not unlike dwarf locusts, and yet not like them, either. Mrs. Plemmons says that Mr. Winn always called them "wild poincianas." She doubts that this is really their name, but who cares? What matters is that this tall, good-natured man of God drove over the rough country roads during the early part of this century, "all the way to Camden County," loaded his old tin lizzie with these bushes which had attracted and cheered him, brought them back to St. Simons, and saw to their planting for several miles on both sides of the little shell road below Christ Church. From what I've heard of Mr. Winn's humor, I wouldn't be at all surprised if he didn't think they'd have his parishioners in a good frame of mind by the time they reached the church, first in their wagons and buggies and later in Model Ts.

No one I know tells a story as graphically as does Lorah Plemmons, and a few minutes ago on the telephone she made me "see" the boys (and as she remembers, also her two daughters, Mary and Sarah) working along with the laughing Mr. Winn, up and down the roadsides, planting his treasure

22

brought "all the way from Camden County."

"The boys," of course, were from the Dodge Home, where Lorah Plemmons kept their young hearts on course for so many years, but I wouldn't be a bit surprised to find out that other Island boys got out of duties at their own homes, because being with Mr. Winn, even armed with hoes and shovels, was so much fun. The creative, happy-natured gentleman has been gone a long time now, but Watson Winn isn't gone at all. Al least until "progress" destroys the roadsides at the north end of St. Simons, he will be around, still bringing a smile to anyone who takes the time to see in late April and early May. Joyce and I never say, "Look, the wild poincianas are blooming." We don't even say, "The bushes Mr. Winn planted are blooming again."

Inevitably, we both exclaim: "Look! Mr. Winn's blooming!"

Anson Dodge left the lovely little church, an architectural jewel nestled among the ancient oaks in Christ Church churchyard. And Watson Winn left his love of life and his flaming spring bushes to remind us that life is to be loved.

To be loved and cherished and guarded and believed in, for all eternity.

# CHAPTER IV

# Dear Mary

While I was away from St. Simons Island on a promotion tour for my novel, *New Moon Rising,* I stood up to speak in a big city hundreds of miles distant, and at one point tears filled my eyes and I had to stop. I was tired, true, but that wasn't the reason. Once again, as I had done all through the exhausting weeks of speaking dates, radio, TV, and press interviews, I was telling the story of how my friend Joyce Blackburn and I happened to own a tiny plot of Christ Church churchyard; how in fact, we "happened" to fall in love with St. Simons Island in the first place.

At an autographing party in Florida, a day or two after our discovery of the Island, a businessman told Joyce that if I meant to do a novel laid on St. Simons, we should look up two people in particular: Mrs. N.C. Young and "the nice warm-hearted lady who is the postmistress on the island." He couldn't remember her name, but as soon as we were able to make it back to St. Simons, they told us in the post office that her name was Mrs. L.W. Everett and that she had retired the day before; that we could talk with her if we just crossed the street and knocked on her door.

Being Yankees then, we hesitated to do that without a telephone call. The jovial man at the post office, whom we now know as our good friend, Fred Heinold, laughed and said, "Call Mrs. Everett? You don't need to do that. She'll be glad to see you!"

He was right. We walked onto her front porch, and before we had a chance to knock, a gracious lady opened the screen door, held out both hands and invited us into her living room—a room now as familiar as our own. She not only walked straight into both our hearts that day, she opened hers to us, and from that moment on, we stopped feeling like visitors on St. Simons Island. Not only did Mary Everett turn out to be the niece of Anna Gould Dodge, one of the main characters in my first novel, *The Beloved Invader*, she became for a long time our closest and dearest Island friend, along with her equally gracious and lovable husband, Dutch, who for years had the only Island grocery store.

Mary Gould Everett drove us up and down every sandy road, pointing out the boundaries of old Black Banks plantation where she was born, giving us her special "Gould guided tour" of Christ Church cemetery, introducing us to the older residents of the Island who might remember her Aunt Anna and her colorful ex-Yankee husband, the Rev. Mr. Anson Greene Dodge. Mary was a little too young to remember much, but her sister, Berta Taylor, and Berta's husband, Douglas, remembered, as did Maud Shadman. Mr. "Cusie" Fleming, Mr. Willis Procter, Captain and Mrs. N.C. Young, Mrs. Lorah Plemmons—the list was long. And daily we "obeyed" our new friend, Mary, when she waved goodbye to us from her shady front porch, calling: "Now,

25

check in again tomorrow, girls! We'll be right here."

She always was and so was Dutch. It was they who began to call us "the Gould girls"—not only flattering where our ages are concerned, but causing us to feel included all the way.

On the platform of the country club where I was speaking that day in the distant city, I came to the part of my story when Mary Gould Everett, with her beloved Dutch in tow, knocked on the door of the beach cottage where Joyce and I lived during the time we were hunting acreage on the island. "Get out your checkbooks, darlin'," Mary caroled, entering our little living room, her arms outstretched as usual. "Dutch and I have just discovered that a man from Albany, who owns the plot between ours and Berta's in Christ Church churchyard, wants to sell it! It's right between where the four of us are going to lie down someday, right in Gould row, and we don't want any outsiders in there. We want you!"

After my audience had laughed warmly at this part of the true story, I had to stop. A few months ago, in the plot to one side of ours, they had buried Mary's sister, Berta. And that day, as I was speaking, they laid Mary on the other side.

*New Moon Rising*, my second novel in the St. Simons trilogy, is the story of Mary's grandfather, Horace Bunch Gould. Somehow, on my feet facing that large audience, I was struck for the first time that not only would Mary never wave to me again from her shady front porch across from the post office, she would never read her grandfather's story, either. My audience grew quiet when I told them. But then a kind of joy overcame me. My beloved friend Mary couldn't read the book, but she was actually with her grandfather that very day! Gratitude replaced my grief. I doubt that many of us ever experience gratitude in its purest form, but I came close as I realized, along with my friend Joyce, that if Mary Gould

Everett hadn't lived just when she did, hadn't opened her door and her heart to us that day we walked unannounced onto her front porch, the chances are we would not have fallen in love with St. Simons, would not be living here now, and without Mary, there might well be no St. Simons trilogy in progress.

It was through Mary that I became so interested and involved with the Gould family. It was through her that I came to believe in them as human beings worth writing about. It was Mary who gave me her only copy of the unpublished family history written by Agnes Hartridge. When the third in the trilogy is completed, I will have spent most of a decade writing about the Goulds of St. Simons Island, Georgia, and I have never spent a more meaningful ten years.

For forty-three years Mary was postmistress at St. Simons, but she was far more than that. She was a friend to everyone, native or tourist, who ever "set foot in her post office," as Dutch was—a friend to everyone, native or tourist, who ever "set foot in his grocery store."

Mainly because Mary Gould Everett was the kind of human being who had never been a stranger to love, no one whose life touched hers could remain a stranger to the island she loved. My heart dictated these inadequate lines, and Mary is still much alive in my grateful heart.

# CHAPTER V

# *Bird Notes*

From any point of view, the most loved, most admired, and most popular "person" in America is Charlie Schultz's Snoopy, the World War One flying ace who, with his helmet firmly strapped under his chin, goggles and scarf in place, searches out and brings down the Red Baron time after time, then relaxes at the officer's canteen over a foaming mug of root beer and imparts to us the thoughts we need to live by.

Life would be almost unbearable without Snoopy. I nearly wrote: "Life would be almost unbearable without Snoopy, the dog." That would have been incorrect. Snoopy is not merely a dog. Not merely a human being. Not merely a philosopher. Not merely a World War One flying ace. He is a composite of us all. I had one of my Snoopy days yesterday.

In a holly tree by our guest house lives a mockingbird we have named Snoopy, who has "Snoopy Days" every day. He is totally human, totally bird, totally neurotic, and totally predictable. Like Snoopy in the comic strip, our winged

Snoopy's very predictability is comforting because he is always predictable in the same ways we are. He handles each crisis, failure or success, with helmet and goggles in place and scarf flying.

He got his name in the first place for being just plain "snoopy." Though his holly-tree residence is at the east end of our house, every night when (in winter) Joyce builds the fire at the end of the workday, while I prepare the "foaming root beer," there, as dependably as the sunset, is Snoopy the mocker, joining the "happy hour" outside the living room sitting on a branch of another holly tree. He cleans his "home" tree of berries, but he never touches the berries on the happy-hour tree! We have no explanation for this, of course, and wouldn't want one. Snoopy is a private bird. The living-room holly tree is his property, and no other winged creature is permitted even to rest there en route to the feeders out back.

This life pattern had been well established before our "snoopy" mocker became Snoopy, the philosopher, the altogether human, quite neurotic warrior of the goggles and helmet and scarf.

After living on St. Simons for a few years, we had become quite familiar with life patterns of mockingbirds, or we thought we had. They are eccentric loners who stake out territories and guard them with valor. They are temperamental artists whose own singing so thrills their very souls that it is not at all unusual to see one "sending" himself straight up in the air from a lamppost or a TV aerial. We know, of course, that mockingbirds sing at night—do some of their most expert Bach and Vivaldi at three in the morning. We know they don't sing all winter, seeming to relish their studied silences as much as their spring arias.

But almost none of this applies to Snoopy. I must tell you that he permits no other mockers within the boundary lines of our four acres. It is time for at least one more mocker of another sex to be around, but she is not! Snoopy reigns alone.

He has been different from any other mockingbird in the whole Southland since the big attack by the Red Baron and his fiendish hordes on the Sunday afternoon of March 16, 1968. This happened to be the first anniversary of our move into our new home. We preferred to spend it alone, with time and quiet really to believe we'd finally made it into what to us is the most wonderful house on the most wonderful spot on earth. Spring training was still in progress, so there wasn't even a Braves baseball game to listen to on the radio. In heavenly seventy-five-degree weather we lounged on our screened back porch, reading. Now and then one of us would say, "Can you really believe we're actually living here? And for a whole year today?"

Except for the usual stinging sounds of the inevitable Sunday planes in the sky overhead, peace was everywhere—inside us and outside. The whitethroats were still here, nibbling seeds on the brick wall near the porch, the red-bellied woodpecker, named Woody Estes, was putting on quite a show hanging upside down at the feeders—none of which was made for him. Cardinals sat like bright blossoms in the ornamental shrubs across our newly planted yard. We had learned not to mind the friendly black snake who lived in the yaupon by the porch. Life was good and whole and full of peace for us both.

Suddenly we jumped at what sounded like the attack of a dozen big hawks. There was a clatter and rattle of wings and a repeated sound we had come to dread, the thud of a flying bird against our windows. We both ran around the corner of

30

the house to the driveway outside the living-room bay. The attack was in progress in Snoopy's holly tree! At least 150 cedar waxwings had wandered by, spotted Snoopy's carefully guarded holly berries, and there he was—goggles in place, helmet strapped under chin, scarf flying, diving, banking, attacking, firing everything he knew to fire at the marauding hordes! Up and down, in and out, over and under, Snoopy fought until the waxwings had punctured his trusty Sopwith Camel with a million holes. Snoopy staggered, fell to the ground, rose again, gave it the gun—did not give up. Did not give up, I cringe to say, until the last waxwing had disappeared because the last berry was gone!

We didn't laugh. We love Snoopy, and we had failed him in his hour of greatest need. How do two mere women fight off a band of hungry waxwings? We didn't know, and so we did all we knew to do: we grieved with Snoopy, tried to tell him the berries would grow back next year, tried to reassure him of our love. Told him over and over that he had done well, had fought the good fight. Singlehanded, he had taken on over 150 of the enemy. True, he had failed, but like us all, he could learn from his failure. Life holds failures for everyone. We all have had our Red Baron hordes.

Snoopy has never been the same since the battle. His personality was altered beyond belief. All over St. Simons Island mockingbirds are singing—have been singing for weeks. Not a note yet from Snoopy. He still comes to happy hour each night, still lives in the holly tree on the opposite end of the house, but hour after hour, day after day, he sits either in his home tree or on the post light, brooding, thinking, trying to discover where it was he failed that Sunday afternoon of March 16, 1968. Oh, he will dive at shrikes, and infrequently at red-winged blackbirds; he nibbles at a piece of proffered raisin bread now and then; but Snoopy has become predictable in an un-mockerish way. He is now an aging veteran of savage combat. A veteran of the Waxwing War where he failed, as those who wage war always fail.

Sometimes when we need special cheering, Snoopy sings a little. We know he will sing a few arias before the summer is over, but only because he loves us and deigns now and then to respond to our need. Last year in May, when I was just about to leave for a much-dreaded promotion tour, at the very hour I was experiencing the deepest depression, Snoopy sang! Several glorious Te Deums—I rallied, took the trip, returned safely, and on my first day back Snoopy sang again. He has been silent ever since, but he is here and he is our mockingbird. If his ghastly war experience has made him neurotic, we try to remember and understand.

*      *      *

A span of time has passed since I wrote the above, and life is filled with stress for Snoopy again. For three days, from twenty to fifty cedar waxwings have been once more "invading" his holly berry crops. Just when we felt he was quieting down, his nerves settling from an invasion of robins in his wild cherry tree several weeks back, his old enemies the waxwings are with us again.

The robin invasion cost Snoopy one dark gray tailfeather, so that when he turns to one side he appears to have a white tail. Temporarily, at least, we have changed his name to Chief White Feather. Unavoidable, I suppose, since I am definitely in my "Indian period" after having read *Bury My Heart at Wounded Knee,* a book every American should be required to read.

Snoopy, for now at least, is as beleaguered as any Indian chieftain, in his desperation to keep his territory out of the reach of the waxwings. Yet the land on which we live and which we call *ours* never "belonged" to the red man, by his standards. It belonged to the Great Spirit; and along came white men, with invasion in their eyes and little measuring rods in their hands and boundary line on their minds. One reading of *Bury My Heart at Wounded Knee* (a documented piece of historical writing, not propaganda) will convince you that it's all the way man looks at the land that matters. To the Indian, his very body was a part of the land on which he lived and hunted. He felt not a sense of ownership but rather one of freedom to use the land in order to live and feed his family and himself. He felt free to wander the earth, an integral part of it all. The white man, with European laws of ownership in his blood, had other ideas. Come to think of it, my analogy was incorrect at the beginning of this column. The waxwings are more like the Indians. Snoopy must be part white Land Baron! He has boundaries and he wants no other worm- or berry-eating birds to cross those lines.

The Guale Indians, who "vacationed," hunting and fishing, on St. Simons Island, did not feel they owned the Island. It was simply there for them to use, to enjoy, to be fed by. Like the waxwings, they came and went with no thought about the trap of time, with thought and movement governed only by the seasons and their needs. The earth was created as the Indian saw it, for man to use, but not to spoil.

I learn a lot from my mocker and from the waxwings and from the Indians whose eloquent, plaintive statements are quoted verbatim in *Bury My Heart at Wounded Knee*. Some days I'd like to be a cedar waxwing, free to wander the sky and

33

the earth, to enjoy and not to possess. Other days I revel in my four acres recorded in the Brunswick Courthouse in my name.

My mockingbird may be peculiar because I am peculiar.

Still most days these words of the Nez Perce chieftain, Heinmot Tooyalaket, haunt me: *The earth was created by the assistance of the sun, and it should be left as it was. . . . The country was made without lines of demarcation, and it is no man's business to divide it.*

Mr. Snoopy Land Baron, are you listening? All that chatter from the flock of cedar waxwings in what you consider *your* holly tree might be making a great amount of sense.

*　　　*　　　*

We should avoid the use of "they" where birds are concerned, as with people. Blacks are not all alike. Chicanos are not all alike. Whites are not all alike. Woodpeckers and mockingbirds and cardinals and painted buntings are not all alike. At least, not around my house.

Surely there cannot be another mockingbird like Snoopy. He began, at the normal time, to dance around about two feet distant from a lady mocker; ate worms with her peaceably in the front lawn throughout April; disappeared for hours at a time from his predictable perch on the front or back yard lamppost or the old magnolia stump left for him in the front lawn. Seemed to be about the "normal" spring business of building a nest for purposes of raising a family. He didn't fool us one bit! He had done this in other springs through which we have lived in the woods. As before, by early May, Snoopy was all alone. Since mid-April or before, mockingbirds had been singing all up and down the island, on Sea Island, in Brunswick. Not Snoopy. He remained silent as a philoso-

34

pher until mid-May! After all, male birds are supposed to sing for mating reasons. Snoopy has chased his mate away in order to be first in our hearts, and to get all the raisins. Now that the mating season is past, he is back on his lamppost singing arias—alone!

Cardinals. Our cardinals, unlike most of the other birds around, are fairly normal in the main. They've built nests, hatched their little ones, worked themselves to small nubs attempting to keep those gaping baby mouths filled. Being monogamous, the papa cardinals (all of whom we call Richelieu) are now feeding mama tenderly, as though to thank her for all she's done to add to the cardinal population at Frederica. But can you believe our cardinals eat azaleas? Around our place, by choice, we have only white azaleas. Whether the color has anything to do with this peculiarity, I don't know. But this spring, our cards, male and female, could be seen at any time of the day eating azalea blossoms: flying upward until they managed to pluck off just the bloom they wanted, then nestling down in the pine straw beneath the bushes, the hapless white flower waving like a little banner from orange beaks—until it disappeared at last inside red throats.

Painted buntings. At Frederica we have them. One could never doubt the Creator's imagination when looking at a male painted bunting. Royal blue head, rosy coral breast, brownish-red wings, and a little bright green shawl across his shoulders. A tiny bird, smaller than most sparrows, but full of fight. Our favorites, I guess, of all the birds who come. We begin listening in early March for the crystal song to fall from the top of some tall pine or tupelo. *The unmistakable bunting song.* Perhaps it, too, is a mating call, because the males appear long before the all-green females, but buntings

35

don't mate all summer long and they do sing all summer long. First, though, there is that time of "listening" early in March. At the enchanted moment when the first notes fall, we stop whatever we're doing and run from one end of the house and yard to the other, armed with field glasses, hoping for just one glimpse of the tiny, bright bird we've missed so all winter long. *He does not show.* He can be singing so near, and we go on trying, but we have never found him yet. Not until he is ready to reward us with that first flash of color at one of our feeders. As I remember, the first shy visit this spring came a week later than last year. Joyce missed it. She was away doing some research. When she called me long-distance that night, the first thing she heard was my shout: "He's here! He's here!" I didn't need to explain that it was Richard, our painted bunting. Now his friends have joined him and the ladies and babies. It will be bright color time in our backyard until late August, when the breath-taking feathers begin to fall out, one by one. The gay green shawl dims first, then the royal blue head, and one day in early September, as though ashamed, our bunting will sneak away. All the way to Panama, one bird book says. And when the last one is gone, we begin right then to wait for spring.

# CHAPTER VI

# A Day of Rest

It is Sunday morning as I write this; still too early to be going to church and a day on which I vowed not to work. I have overworked this year, unintentionally, of course, but publisher's deadlines do not wait. At least, they do not wait if one earns one's living by writing books. I had declared today a holiday for me because I thought I needed it. I would sleep late, feed my birds, sit on the back porch in the sun, think, rest. Really rest.

But here I am up before seven, sitting where I've sat for most of the year, banging on my typewriter. I think I was inspired last night. One of my friends, Clara Marie Gould (a descendant of the people I have come to love in my St. Simons trilogy of novels) came for dinner. She had just finished reading my manuscript of her great-great-grandfather's story, *Lighthouse*. Clara Marie liked it so much, in no time she had me feeling as though I'd slept for a week and hadn't worked a day all year. For hours we talked about James Gould, the builder of the first St. Simons lighthouse, about politics and the assorted children she teaches every day of the week at Goodyear Elementary School. (I'm still gasping, by the way, to learn that in our hot climate, the schools are not air-conditioned, and last night I learned that not only do our long-suffering teachers have to attempt to keep wiggly youngsters at attention during 90- and 95-degree weather, the gnats swarm through the open windows and dig their ways into the scalps of teacher and pupils. Clara Marie, being Clara Marie, merely makes a good story of it—laughs and increases my admiration for all teachers who care in a creative way about teaching.)

I rode out to my gate with her at midnight, strolled back to the house in moonlight as clear as day, and hated myself for frightening away two deer grazing in my front yard. The woods on St. Simons and Frederica by moonlight banish the years for me. There are few planes in the air at night. Where I live no cars can drive by. The clock turns back, and my trees throw the same shadows the trees cast on the famous rose garden at James Gould's New St. Clair plantation in 1820 and 1830, and I neither snap on my flashlight nor hurry, but linger along my winding shell road, white, white under the full moon hanging over the small back marsh, and I wish, as I have wished so many times since I've lived here, that one didn't have to waste time sleeping.

Off to my left, somewhere along the margin of the big marsh that stretches west toward Brunswick, a night animal rattled its way through the dry leaves and palmetto; from the woods to the east, I heard my first chuck-will's-widow of the year, and tired as I am supposed to be, I found myself wishing morning would come so that I could begin another day on St. Simons Island—a day that would be filled with the songs of shouting birds and sunlight and shadow, and the longed-for solitude I so revere and love. That's one of the problems of life in coastal Georgia for me. There I stood in my lane, reveling in the night-sounds and the clean, white moonlight turning my shingle roof silver—wanting to hold every night-moment forever and at the same time impatient for the dawn and another day. None of this means I don't have hectic, exhausting days with too many calls, too many angles to figure, too much mail left unanswered. Days that seem to dig even deeper than Golden Isles gnats and sandflies.

But do you know what gets me through these prickly times with more success than anything else I've tried? Our birds. Both Joyce and I (except on rare occasions) begin our days watching our birds. I understand that we now have fewer varieties than in the years past, but at least we can't complain about the numbers. All winter long, the minute the back door opens, it is as though a celestial sling were released as more than a hundred "regular customers," cardinals, white-throated sparrows, towhees, song sparrows, blue jays, doves, and red-winged blackbirds zoom out of the woods and from the marsh margins and literally "bloom" up and down our old dead oak out back, pushing and shoving one another for perching space on the wisteria vine which now covers its empty branches. Who says birds have "bird brains"? The sound of that back door and Joyce's voice calling: "Is anyone hungry out here?" fills the air with wings. Even our eccentric and altogether unpredictable mockingbird, Snoopy, eases in toward the top of one feeder where he knows breadcrumbs and a handful of raisins will be left for him..

The latest on Snoopy is that he has a "friend." Whether this friend is male or female, I cannot say. Who can say with mockingbirds? But other mockers are nesting and singing on St. Simons Island and in Brunswick and the neighboring

39

Golden Isles. Not Snoopy. He is still creeping about, now and then doing his little dance with his "friend," then flying off on some secret mission of his own. We were galvanized the other day to hear one small experimental phrase—unmistakably Snoopy. Then silence. Every other male is shouting with joy or bravado or whatever it is that opens their winter-locked throats in the spring as they stake out their claims. But not Snoopy. He really needs a psychiatrist, we're certain. After yesterday, no doubt remains. Some late robins stopped off in our front yard and, unlike his daily performance for the past month or so, Snoopy went about his mysterious "hunting" as though the robins hadn't invaded his private lawn. He has chased off three families of bluebirds since we've lived here and refuses to permit any worm- and bug-eating bird to linger long—except, of course, Georgia's haughty state bird, the brown thrasher, who bows to neither man nor mocker. But so help me, Snoopy pretended those robins hadn't come yesterday! And more peculiar than that, he managed to overlook two flickers at work in the same "mocker territory."

But then, our birds all seem rather peculiar, at least, if one takes the Peterson *Field Guide to Birds* seriously—or any other book in which mere man attempts to predict the habits and mores of these free-winging creatures. We are told by the bird-book authors and our friends here that blue jays, for instance, are fussy and mean. Oh, ours make those fussy sounds, broken now and then by pure flutelike calls, and when they land, they come in so hard and fast they bounce. And since they are large, the other birds make room for them. But not once have we seen our jays fight another bird or even each other. Towhees, the lovely ground robins with the soft, distinctive spring calls, are supposed never to sit in trees, according to one authority. He hasn't observed our

40

towhees. I had my breakfast coffee today on the back porch and watched a male towhee sing for twenty minutes in the top of the old wisteria-covered oak!

Male hummingbirds always drive off the females once the spring job is done, one reads, but not our male humming-birds. Ours, like Snoopy, are, year after year, unorthodox. The male hummer is more attractive, and we wish the atmosphere of our place didn't cause these quirks among them. I sit on Lorah Plemmons's porch and watch her male drive off every female hummingbird. I come back here and catch one quick glimpse of the ruby throat, and zoom! the poor fellow is speared by a less attractive female and never permitted near the sugar water again that day.

The normally docile female cardinals are also exponents of Women's Lib about this time of year. The cards are all nesting, of course, and it exhausts me to think about it. For two years, we have lost working time and worn ourselves out watching the agonizing period of feeding and the ultimate agony of pushing the scrawny babies out of the nest. This year, I'm almost thankful to say, neither of us has located an active cardinal's nest. I've just finished a novel. I'm too tired to go through it again, so I hope we don't find one.

Some of our birds, the cardinals in particular, appear to be quite normal in their psyches, and it is rather a relief. Writers are supposed to be kooky people, a fact we don't deny, but we would hate to feel we had exerted a strong influence on our feathered performers. I just think birds are somewhat like people. You can no more glibly say "they" with birds than with people.

I didn't mean to write this today, as I said, but writing for me is much like gossip for some persons—a disease. An especially springtime disease. After all, the birds are busy creating; what's wrong with a writer writing on her day of rest?

# CHAPTER VII

# Try Looking in the Rain

I hear from folk who have visited St. Simons for a few days—St. Simons, Sea Island, Jekyll, Brunswick—and the letters are sometimes one long moan of sadness or complaint.

Sample:

"We had waited so long to see St. Simons Island, to walk around the little churchyard at Frederica, hoping it would all look as you describe it in your novels, etc. But, alas, it rained both days we were there!"

Well, I suppose if walking or lying in the sun is what you want from a vacation, or several hours on a golf course under the sun, rain would spoil it all for you. But who wears good clothes on a vacation to a little island? I mean if you're looking for the beauties of our natural environment in the Golden Isles, if you really want to stand beside a big live oak and revel in its wide, spreading branches covered with resurrection ferns and ivy—if you really want to walk in Christ churchyard—now, will you be wearing a suit or a

43

dress which the rain can spoil?

I admit sometimes we have heavy summer downpours, but generally they are ephemeral. Almost always, by sundown the clouds are tossing tall and white again, the sun picking out whole spectrums of color in a drop of water trapped on the point of a palmetto frond. Put on some old clothes and live it up in the rain!

I consider it too bad if a first time visitor from another part of the country comes to see me and some rain doesn't fall. Winter rains are another thing, I agree. They can go on for three or four days, cold and blowy. But summer rains? I love them. If fact, if you spend all your vacation in the Golden Isles and miss a good, soaking thunderstorm, you've missed seeing some of the most breath-taking sights.

People have a peculiar idea of "good weather" anyway. Do you realize that just three or four days of sun causes our singular resurrection ferns, which grow along the branches of the live oaks and on the brick wall and tombstones at Christ Church, to dry and curl, so that if you are here without a rain, you'll miss them? I am constantly amazed at how few Islanders know and appreciate resurrection ferns. Someone told me once that she had lived here for fifteen years and until she read about resurrection ferns in one of my novels, she had never noticed them! Another friend confessed, after reading my *Illustrated* columns on our thinned-out Spanish moss, that he had not noticed it was almost gone!

In the rain, Spanish moss turns soft, lovely green, so don't feel gypped if it rains on your vacation. Hunt a woodsy spot and examine a strand of live, green moss. No two clumps grow exactly the same way. Moss is free-form and clean, and it grows in an almost random pattern.

Yes, in the rain, Spanish moss turns grayish green, and

44

resurrection ferns stand up within a couple of hours, and if you walk or drive up and down our roads—all except those marked *private*, of course—you'll find a wonderland of lichen springing up in flowerlets and lace and curls along our tree trunks, branches, and even covering dead twigs that have fallen to the ground. Last week friends gave a party for me to celebrate both my birthday and the completion of *Lighthouse*, my current novel. It rained and I was delighted! Of course, we stayed inside mostly, but the doors were open to the wide porches, and the rain didn't last long. But oh, the small, surprising beauties I found as I walked slowly to my car!

Dead oak twigs had fallen and lay bright green and pink in fresh lichen and wet, sparkling moss. I walked maybe fifty yards, I filled my hands with fairyland treasures.

Drive to the churchyard at Frederica when it's raining and look up into the trees. Then examine the brick wall out front. And take deep, deep breaths of clean, washed, salty air, sweetened by leaf mould and wet pin needles.

It's thundering right now. And I'm glad. Earlier today when I walked down my lane to the mailbox, I noticed my two guarded patches of resurrection fern were beginning to dry up.

Rain can't spoil a vacation in the Golden Isles if you keep your sense of humor revved up and your eyes open to the magnificent microcosm that is a "golden isle." The big view is stunning. Sun is great. But there is surprising beauty in the small things, too. Try looking in the rain.

# CHAPTER VIII

# *The Light at Christmas*

I am leaving St. Simons tomorrow. It won't be easy. It will be my first Christmas away from the Island since Joyce and I came here in 1961. My mother and her neighbor, Nancy Goshorn, have always come to me for Christmas. Mother's broken leg is mended; she is managing quite elegantly with a cane now and could probably make the trip. But I have business in New York, Savannah, and Atlanta; and this year it will be simple to stop with Mother in West Virginia.

I awoke today just as the sun rose above the small marsh back of our house, and I stood, as I do almost every morning at my bedroom window, just looking and wondering at the light. Few days have passed since I've lived here when I haven't wondered at the always changing Island light. The marshes around my house turn from deep black-brown to tawny wheatfield gold as the sun slides across the sky. But early morning is different, especially on the small back marsh to the east. This morning's light took my breath away! We

47

had stood on the back porch in the dark last night listening—literally listening—to the dew fall from the branches of the trees, and at sunrise this morning it clung to every blade of spartina grass, breaking the sunlight into so many splinters of light, I could almost not bear to look. One thinks of words (or tries to) having to do with jewels, the facets of a diamond, a sapphire, ruby, topaz, emerald, especially when a drop of dew fractures the light into the rainbow colors of a prism. But all of these words are inadequate. On a cloudy day, beautiful as it remains, spartina grass is mainly brown. It is the Island light which works the magic; which clarifies, outlines, throws into deep shadows, alters even the shapes of familiar trees and bushes.

I am looking now out my office window toward the woods in front of my house. One giant live oak with a rugged, crooked elbow is almost out of sight. This afternoon, when the light moves, it will stand out and appear twice its size. Right now, where the sunlight strikes, a small water oak and a slender black gum are the attention-getters. When I look up quickly, I see those two average-sized trees first. The big live oak is in shadow, except for a large white dapple of light halfway down the rough trunk.

Light picks out. Selects. Brings forward. Clarifies. It also dims, blots out.

The light on the back marsh early this morning blotted out the trees along Plantation Point, where my neighbors, the Albert Fendigs, live. It was as though even their tall white house had vanished. This evening their picturesque tree line and the handsome roofline will come back.

It has occurred to me that when I have to be away from St. Simons, I miss most the changing Island light.

Light has always fascinated and mystified me. White light

48

isn't white. The colors of the rainbow are always there. All those colors make white light. It may be just as well that we don't see rainbows often. They'd lose their wonder. But in a sense, they're always there. And not always in the traditional arc of color, either. On the beach one day, Joyce and I decided not to hurry away from a swiftly coming storm. We strolled along through the big raindrops and watched the sky. I hope you've seen this before, but we hadn't. There, among the turbulent dark gray clouds, hung one lone cloud—not white, as we think of white, but suspended at just the right place to break up the light into every color of the rainbow. It was not an arc of color. A moment before, the cloud had been white. Before our eyes, the magic came, lingered for two or three minutes, then vanished. During those minutes we wanted to shout to all the hurrying swimmers and sunbathers: "Look up! Look Up! Look at what the light is doing to that cloud in the sky!"

Christmas on St. Simons Island is a time of changing light. The now familiar, clear, winter light along the coast has come to be as Christmasy to me as snow was for all the years of my life before I found St. Simons. The cassina and pyracantha and holly berries are redder because of that Christmas light. Words grow stubborn here, because in this special winter light, there is a quality of eternity for me. The Great Going On becomes even more believable. God would have to be a fiend to have created us with the capacity to revel in His changing light, if one last earthly breath could blot it out forever!

I will miss the Island light this year, but being away from it, having it out of my physical sight, will not bring darkness. The snow may fly in my hometown and in New York while I'm there, and the gray clouds may hover, but this year I intend to concentrate more deeply than ever before on my favorite Christmas verses from the Gospel of John. Not the traditional Bethlehem verses, although I love those, too. But to me John, the disciple Jesus loved, wrote the eternal Christmas story. The Baby in the Manger grew up. The first night of Christmas ended. The shepherds and the wise men went home. The *light* from that night will never end.

> In the beginning was the Word, and the Word was with God, and the Word was God. He was in the beginning with God; all things were made through him, and without him was not anything made that was made. In him was life, and the life was the light of men. The light shines in the darkness, and the darkness has not overcome it.

This Word, this Jesus Christ, whose very life is light, became flesh on the first Christmas. Literally became one of us. Got into the mess with us. Is still here, being light for us. On the Bethlehem of Judea night, this "true light that enlightens every man" was coming into the world for the first time.

To stay.

# CHAPTER IX

# Wonder and Sacrilege

This past week one of the country's best-known men in his field, Georgia's state archeologist, Dr. Lewis H. Larson, Jr., came to our Island to certify what many of us believed to be the foundation of St. Simons' first light tower, built by James Gould in the early 1800s. Of course, when one lives through more than a decade with a family, as I've "lived" with the Goulds of St. Simons, an unexplainable attachment is born—unexplainable, perhaps, to anyone who has not shared the absorbing, traumatic, stimulating, back-aching work of writing historical novels.

Dr. Larson and his helpers uncovered the octagonal shape of James' tower, and as I stood watching the tabby and red English sandstone construction appear before my eyes, I wanted to hug each person who lifted a shovel of dirt one careful, cautious scoop after another. I didn't hug them, of course. It was too hot, but I don't think any one doubted my enthusiasm.

My novel manuscript, *Don Juan McQueen*, had gone by

the board all week. I managed only to keep up with a few telephone calls and my mail. I was in my car and down Frederica Road to the lighthouse every free moment.

The second day Dr. Larson's crew worked, I insisted that Joyce go with me. She took one quick look into the "digs," turned, and ran to the St. Simons Library, shouting back: "I've got to tell Fraser Ledbetter and Lillian Knight!" On her way she stopped off at the St. Simons Chamber of Commerce to tell Jean Alexander. Those were three people she knew would be as excited and gratified as we were.

And every day during the excavation, Weyman Huckabee and Willis Warnell were always there when I arrived, standing in the sun, as excited as schoolboys with the finding of every old nail, every rusty length of chain, every broken piece of pottery, every glass fragment of what we believe to have been the lantern globes. Even a child's large stone marble was found on the floor of the old tower. To me, of course, this had to have belonged to Horace Gould (the main character of my novel, *New Moon Rising*), who was a small boy when his daddy built the first St. Simons light.

The excavation is still uncovered as I write this, but by the time you read it, the county will have filled it in again. If not, Dr. Larson stressed, "the elements would disintegrate the fine plaster job on the outside of the tower and people would carry the ruins off piece by piece." Sad though, covering it up, but only with sand and sod, so if the glorious day comes when our Coastal Georgia Historical Society can afford proper protection of the valuable ruins, uncovering them again will not be difficult.

On the subject of the difficulty of such excavations, this seems the right time to extend my heartfelt thanks to the likable and diligent young men sent by the county to follow

Dr. Larson's instructions. Keith McDowell and Johnnie Howe were the two regulars. Each worked as carefully and cleanly as an experienced "digger" for treasure, even though I'm sure neither young man had ever done archeological excavation before.

Working equally as well and as hard were Ricky Gunn and Rob Owens. All four of these fellows really impressed me. They confirmed my often-attacked confidence in our young people. Daily I could see their involvement increase. They had aching backs at night (along with magnificent tans), but historical sites will never, never be just "a pile of ruins" to them again.

But the wonder was almost spoiled when, on the first day of excavation, someone came running to Dr. Larson to tell him that bulldozers had destroyed an Indian burial ground on what had once been James Gould's plantation along Frederica Road. Immediately, Lewis Larson and his assistant, Marilyn Pennington, a graduate student in archeology from the University of Georgia, went to the scene. Broken bones and crushed skulls lay in a ghastly, useless heap. I missed all this, but Dr. Larson was heartbroken when he told me about it.

"History in this or any area in Georgia belongs to all Georgians," he said, his normally quiet voice trembling a little as he spoke. "It's a sacrilege!"

I looked from his troubled face to Keith McDowell and Johnnie Howe, who were cautiously unearthing more fragile glass fragments from the base of the lighthouse. These two young men, at least, will never be casual and careless of Georgia's treasures, I thought.

Seeing James Gould's lighthouse foundation filled me with wonder, but I'm still a little ill at the thought of that destroyed Indian midden at the site of James Gould's old home.

53

St. Simons Light and Keepers House

# CHAPTER X

# No Pat Answers

This has been a busy summer of fund-raising and plans for the exciting restoration of the lightkeeper's house, now the museum of our own Coastal Georgia Historical Society.

I have also been trying to put together the utter chaos of historical intrigue along the Florida-Georgia border back in the year 1792, which must, if I'm to keep my sanity, be untangled for the writing of my next novel. It is a time of delight and despair over the shaky fortunes of my favorite baseball team, the Atlanta Braves, of trying to stay no more than a month behind my mail, of keeping up with the new crop of painted buntings, cardinals, jays, woodpeckers, lizards, and even snakes. I'd almost forgotten the content of a new book manuscript written toward the end of the last year. As usual, when one is busiest on another project, galley proofs come sailing in, requested back to the publisher "yesterday" in order to make an early fall publishing date.

I've just had the rather interesting experience of rereading in galleys what I had written in this short and, I hope, helpful book. If it helps no one else, the rereading did a lot for me. Perhaps God gave me the idea out of my own need. He does that now and then, you know.

The little book is titled: *No Pat Answers*. I tend to want them, just as I'm sure you do. When our hearts break at a sudden tragedy, an illness discovered overnight, they cry, these hearts of ours, *why*? Someone give me an answer! Why? Why did this terrible thing have to happen to me? to her? to him?

I have had reasons to cry out for an explanation from someone, somewhere, because of one or two distressful events of this busy summer. No big tragedy has occurred in my own life, but in lives very close to mine there have been tragic deaths and illnesses, disappointments, failures, mis-understandings; and since I'm a member of the human race and impatient at best, I need to read my own book.

My friend Joyce tells me now and then that my books, some of them at least, would help *me* if I'd read them. We all go too fast. We all see clearly at times, and then, because we have been going too fast and doing too much, we forget, and the clear, revealing light of our comprehension dims.

I'm behind with my new novel, about six months behind where I should be at this date. I must make a trip north for ten days. It is not only the heart-smashing, enormous tragedies which cause us to shout *Why?* at heaven; more frequently it is the accumulation of small, daily, nitty-gritty occurrences. What I had planned and longed for above all this summer was a reasonably uninterrupted period in which to begin the writing of what will be the most difficult book I've ever tackled. The historical intrigue is just that: *intrigue*.

Intrigue is never simple. Historical intrigue (which I hope will not sound like a textbook account when I've finished at last)

56

is even more complex. As of this writing, I've done twenty-one versions of a prologue which I've (just today) decided not to use! To throw away. Okay. I'm accustomed to that. Even fairly decent books are not written, they're *rewritten*.

I now know I will not make my December deadline. Which only means I'll have to borrow money from my publisher, because the publication of the next novel will be pushed up to spring of 1974 unless there is a miracle. I don't count on them. I see nothing in God's nature which tends to pamper us, to make us weak.

Soon I must pack to leave. The novel? It's in its most confusing mess to date, spread all over my office, and Chapter One is not finished.

So much for the chance details of my own need for today. The point of all this? I needed to reread what I've written in my own earlier manuscript. When I wrote *No Pat Answers* the time was winter, the weather was gray, the house was cozy, the tourists (bless them) were not writing quite so many letters or extending so many warm but impossible invitations. My mind was free. I was quiet inside. I could think. There were no organizational meetings, and there were few telephone calls.

Here is the short passage which has just calmed me, has just reminded me that although there is no "pat answer" to any dilemma, there is always the potential of inner quiet and certainty:

> In the first throes of tragedy (or daily chaos), we rush at God with our questions and firmly believe that He welcomes them. Indeed, I imagine He expects them. After all, no one but God knows us as we really are inside. Still, when we get back only what we, in our sorrow, fear, or panic, recognize as

silence, what of that? Is that all we can expect from "the God of all comfort"? It may be all we can expect by way of *understanding* the reason for our grief, shock, or fear. Could this be where we make our big mistake? Do we fall victim to *time* itself? Do we rush at God in our extremity, demanding an immediate answer in understandable words, not according to God's time schedule, but because we want our question answered now with a pat answer? Explicit, in a manner we can grasp without much concentration? . . . (Yet) how could we expect to be able to hear the voice of God in our distress when we have long ago forgotten, or never learned, to be quiet before Him? . . . There is no time element involved in divine mystery, but there is silence in it. And we can't bear silence. We fear it. The radio or TV is flipped on the minute most of us enter a room. Yet we are told that the voice of God is "a still, small voice." He waits for our inner-silence before He speaks on any subject. Possibly because He wants what He says to be heard. . . .

In the midst of the always chaotic start of a new novel, in the midst of some needed organizational "hecticity," in the midst of packing to be away for almost two weeks, with my heart and mind chained on St. Simons to the still unsolved problem of the new book, I am again quiet inside. No longer demanding a "pat answer" to the question of: Why *this* summer? We must do all we can to preserve the quiet and the peace of the history of our lovely Island. I mean, certainly, to do no less than *all I can*. But even the quiet of a silent oak will pass us by if we are too rushed to stand beneath it for a moment in the silence.

# CHAPTER XI

# I Am a Baseball Nut

Summer is coming. And the reason I know summer is coming is that at West Palm Beach, right now, the men who will control the mood of my summer are running around in circles, doing push-ups, fielding grounders, hitting fungoes, trying to cut out sweets, and complaining about sore muscles.

The noble Atlanta Braves have begun spring training!

I am not a sports fan per se. I couldn't tell you for the life of me what the men who choose to roll and tumble in the mud and rain, grabbing frantically at each other's legs, did all fall with what they call a football; nor could I tell you, if my life depended on it, what those elongated, skinny men in old-fashioned bathing suits did during what is known as basket-ball season. But baseball? That's another thing.

Spring training time, since I was five years old, has been the beginning of the New Year for me. I don't know one golf club from another, although I try to be proud that I live near Brunswick, Georgia, THE HOME OF STEVE MELNYK.

But let the sports pages begin to slip in a baseball story now and then come February and March, and my blood races.

When I was ten, I badgered my patient father until he brought in a crew of men to scrape and prepare a tennis court in the lot next to our house, then I lost interest in tennis before the men finished the court. We planted grass. But baseball? Not once, even during the twelve years or so when I was carrying a top-heavy speaking schedule, have I been "away" from the glorious game—at least in my thoughts.

For years I could tell you every fielding and batting average in the National League and every pitcher's record. My love affair with baseball had to be just that—a love affair—because until I came to live in the South, I was a Chicago Cubs fan. For over twenty-five years I was a Chicago Cubs fan, and during that period, if my memory serves, my beloved Cubbies won maybe a couple of hundred games. (Of course, and I mention this only in the cause of honesty, the minute I moved to St. Simons Island and began to be a rabid Atlanta Braves fan, the Cubbies began to act like men!) But to have been a Cub fan all those years meant one had to be a baseball fan-atic. Like my father, I was. I am.

And now, down there in West Palm Beach, Florida, my men, my noble, upstanding, talented men, are hard at work—for me. This is the marvel of baseball, which no other game will ever replace for good old squares like me. All summer long, baseball will be here. It will be like a friend come home to me. Joyce Blackburn and I will do our level best to permit *nothing* to interfere with listening to play-by-play accounts of the fates of our beloved friends, the noble Braves.

We will plan our work from opening game to the World Series. (*Through* the World Series, because I'm sure Atlanta will take it all this year. I'm always sure of that every

60

February and March.) We will plan our work so we won't have to leave our boys alone to fend for themselves for a single inning. We will yell and shout and cheer and blast them with all the love and caring we can muster. Before each game, we stand and sing the *Star-Spangled Banner* with variations, free to let our voices soar, since we live almost surrounded by the Marshes of Glynn. Sometimes when we're listening to the Braves broadcast on the back porch, our birds scatter into the marshes as we let go our first "Oh, say can you see . . . ." But they come back and join us for the game. At least until the first Braves home run, when our sudden applause and whoops send them scurrying again.

Yes, it's spring training at West Palm Beach. Oh, there are other major-league teams working out too, in other places, according to the papers, but they don't count. Only the Atlanta Braves count, and they are all my favorite players. Rico Carty, the most lovable and colorful "character" in modern baseball, is my top favorite, but they are all best, and they are all best because they are all Atlanta Braves.

Rico and the great Hank Aaron and Pat Jarvis and Ron Reed and Felix Millan and Clete Boyer and Phil Niekro and Milt Pappas and Cecil Upshaw and Bob Didier and Orlando Cepeda and Sonny Jackson and Bob Aspromonte and Tony Gonzales and some new faces I'll learn quickly to love are all preparing my summer for me. I'll be writing a novel between games, but it won't interfere with baseball.

Yes, my boys—the Champs of the Western Division—are hard at work at West Palm Beach. They are running and doing push-ups and dieting and trying with all their courageous hearts to help me forget those black, tragedy-scarred days last fall when suddenly and for no reason whatever, the nation's newspapers were full of some sort of gibberish about

61

a team from Yankeeland called the Mets. I'm through with Yankeeland, myself, and it won't take three innings of the opening game between my magnificent men and whatever luckless team that faces them to forget not only the ignominy of those tragic playoff days but the long fall and winter without a single word of news about my Atlanta Braves.

The wrench of loving baseball is that we live with and for those lovely lads for more than six months of the year. They become close friends. Work schedules are made to conform to their activities, and then it is over. Sportswriters who glowed and suffered with them all summer suddenly find their very names obnoxious. Silence falls. The long winter sets in. They are the same as dead.

But now the men are exercising, spring training has begun, and so has life again.

I am working now night and day to fit together the assorted research materials I have collected so that I can begin to plot my novel. I really am terribly busy these days, but the incentive is at hand. It is all joy to work hard now, during spring training, because soon, oh, soon an umpire will bellow: "Play ball!" and the fun will begin. Work will not seem like work.

Two of our closest Island friends, Mr. and Mrs. F.P. Vanstory, will become an even more integral part of our lives. You see, they are religious about the Braves, too. At the close of every game—on the last out—if the Braves have won, our telephone rings, and we answer not with *Hello* but with a Brave war whoop! Burney Vanstory is whooping on the other end of the line. If the Braves lose, Burney's husband, Van, who has more savvy than Paul Richards in our "humble dogmatic opinion," solemnly reviews Manager Luman Harris's mistakes from A to Z. We share a moment's sorrow by way of Southern Bell and then, as though on cue, we rally. There will be another game tomorrow. Baseball fans don't have to wait a week. And always we know the Braves will take 'em next time.

Right now, I'm convinced this is going to be a spring and summer of whooping along those telephone lines. After all, our splendid Braves are already hard at work for us.

Happy New Year, Atlanta Braves!

*A 1981 Postscript:*

As I write, the winds of February are whipping the moss on my trees, but I am "living in the sunshine." In a little over three weeks, Joyce and I will be at Atlanta Braves Spring Training, baseball caps in place, hot dogs in hand. My doctor suggested the south of France for my prescribed annual month's rest. I could no more endure being in the south of France during Spring Training than I could endure the thought of a baseball strike. Our splendid manager, Bobby Cox, is saying what all Braves' hearts shout: "Wait 'til this year!" He's right, of course. After all, Hrabosky and Garber pitched fine winter ball; my favorite, Larry Bradford, will be ready out of the bullpen; Rick Camp could get no better; immortal Phil Niekro and Elder Gaylord Perry will start, followed by the youngsters, McWilliams, Matula and Boggs. The big bats of Murphy, Horner and Chambliss will boom; Claudell Washington will run; Nahorodny, Benedict, and maybe even Pocoroba will help Ramirez, Gomez and Hubbard seal us "up the middle," and if Matthews and Royster and Asselstine and Miller are around, and with Ernie Johnson's play-by-play, how can we lose? Also, how can I *"wait 'til this year"*?

# CHAPTER XII

# An Unforgettable Man

When Joyce and I first found St. Simons Island, one of the first persons we met—as soon as I had determined to write the novel about the history of Christ Church Frederica—was Mr. Watson Glisson. Mr. Glisson had been the sexton at Christ Church for many years when we met him and for us, as for thousands of tourists from all over America and Canada, he was an integral part of the historic old church and cemetery.

Because of his singular sense of humor and earthy imagination, Mr. Glisson and Joyce and I became fast friends. One of the first things we remember his saying went something like this: "Well, now, I'll tell you ladies something. The Civil War is over. It's been fought and maybe nobody won. But it's over and folks from the North [as we were then] are just as welcome here as they can be!" In no time at all, we sensed that this was no usual caretaker. His quiet, folksy manner and peppery speech were foolers. We soon discovered he was widely read; and more than that,

64

Watson Glisson knew what he'd read. He knew the Bible, as my grandmother used to say, from "kivver to kivver." He and I spent hours trying to "catch" each other on one Scripture passage or another. He caught me often. I never caught him once!

One of Watson Glisson's favorite pastimes was to have a little harmless fun with the tourists who came to Christ Church with all sorts of mixed-up historical "facts" all the way from the Wesleys to the present day in the rather fabulous history of the little church. Until I began digging for material about the Rev. Anson Green Phelps Dodge, Jr., who rebuilt Christ Church in 1884 (in memory of his bride, who died on their honeymoon), little was available about Mr. Dodge except through Watson Glisson. He caught me one day on one of his favorite tourist jokes and after my novel about the church, *The Beloved Invader*, was published in 1965, he "caught" hundreds of tourists who poured into the cemetery with their copies under their arms.

One day Mr. Glisson took me to the other side of Frederica Road across from the church and showed me an old rusty hitching ring, grown now rather high up in an ancient tree.

"You see that ring up there?" he asked, squinting wisely. "Well, that's where Mr. Dodge used to tie John Wesley!"

I had learned by then that it wasn't very smart to show too much surprise and so I tried not to. In a minute, he grinned and said: "I never told anybody this before, but seein' that you're going to write a book about it, the truth of that joke is this. Mr. Dodge called his horse John Wesley!"

Of course, I used that bit of fine information in the novel.

I used that and many, many other pertinent facts gleaned with Watson's help, from the markers in the cemetery, and in the church itself. If he and I happened to be alone in the sanctuary with no tourists about, he would let me behind the chain that closes off the front of the church on weekdays, so that I could locate just the spot in the floor where Ellen Dodge, Anson's bride, had been buried until she was moved at his death to the Dodge plot outside to the rear and side of the church. Watson Glisson showed me where the addition had been built onto the little building after Mr. Dodge's death. He explained that the small white marble statue at the rear of the church was placed there by Anson Dodge's mother also after his death.

"Italian white marble that is," Mr. Glisson whispered confidentially. "She had it made when she and the little fellow traveled in Italy when he was eight or ten years old. I don't reckon Mr. Dodge would've allowed that to be on display like that while he was alive, but there he sits now! Mr. Dodge himself at the age of eight or ten."

He showed me a stained-glass window where one of the figures has a thumb with three joints; he had a trick way of moving the swinging sanctuary door so the large back window placed there in Anson Dodge's memory reflected like a movie projector on another wall and seemed to be moving under its own power when Watson caught the light just right and swung the door slowly.

During his tenure at Christ Church, he enlightened me and thousands of other people with a hundred and one oddments of Glisson; colorful information, but most of all, Watson Glisson was a kind, warm-hearted man as much at home spinning a tall tale or reading a book as whirling around the spacious churchyard on his tractor-lawnmower.

"I can see Christ Church churchyard as though I were right there today," a lady said to me last spring on the West Coast. "I will never forget that beautiful setting under those

66

Christ Church-Frederica

massive oaks, but I will also never forget the sexton, Mr. Glisson!" And she hadn't been on St. Simons Island for over eight years.

Some months ago, a younger man came to take over Mr. Glisson's beloved job. My longtime friend had given in at last to chronic bronchitis and emphysema, aggravated by his long, faithful years spent in all kinds of weather in the damp, sometimes chill beauty of the churchyard at Frederica. I had heard he had been taken to Rome, Georgia, for examination and treatment. Then I saw him on Frederica Road in his car one day, but only two days ago did I learn where my friend is now. And yesterday, I visited him.

Watson Glisson, one of the most independent, joke-loving, informative outdoor gentlemen I've met on St. Simons Island, is in Room 18E at the Brunswick Nursing and Convalescent Center. As soon as I learned his whereabouts, I hurried across the marshes and found him lying on his bed, his once-ruddy face pale from the weeks inside four walls. On the little bedside table stood a framed picture of the place he loves most on earth: Christ Church Frederica.

We just plain hugged each other. He wasn't any happier over our reunion than I was.

# CHAPTER XIII

# A Very Special Book

I am writing this on a soft, sunny day, a handsomely designed and jacketed new book open beside my typewriter. I'd like very much to share the author's inscription to me:

> For Eugenia—
> This, my eighth book, is the most
> meaningful to us for obvious reasons.
> I am grateful for all those reasons.
>    Joyce
> Frederica,
>          September, 1970

The new book, which has so much meaning, is the latest written by my dear friend, Joyce Blackburn, with whom I found St. Simons Island. The title of the book is *James Edward Oglethorpe*. Joyce is right: "for obvious reasons" this one in particular has deep meaning for us both. As with most tourists, the Island's marvelous Fort Frederica National Monument was, after Christ Church, one of the real attractions to us on that first day here back in 1961, when Frederica Road was still an over-arching wonder of woods and tangled vines almost all the way from the airport to the fort.

Driving north on Frederica Road, we first came to Christ Church, and by noon of that glorious day I had decided to write a novel about its builder—another Yankee who had fallen under the Island's spell—the Rev. Anson Green Phelps Dodge, Jr.

Our next stop around the beautiful wooded curve in the road was Fort Frederica, and after our initial delight at finding so much condensed history to explore in such an unexpected place came our shock at how little we both really knew about the man named James Edward Oglethorpe. Of course we remembered his name in connection with the founding of the colony of Georgia, but beyond that and a dim recollection of some people called Salzburgers, two young English clerics named Wesley, and Oglethorpe's unusual respect for Indians, we knew almost nothing.

"It must be that we had a lopsided Yankee education," Joyce remarked. We knew about Jamestown and Boston and Philadelphia.

Now, having been Islanders for most of ten years, we are not so sure it was altogether the fault of Yankee-slanted history in our youth. At a luncheon given by our publishers in Atlanta almost two years ago, Joyce was literally besieged by the state's leading librarians and educators to "give us a short, accurate, colorful biography of Oglethorpe." Even Georgians knew little about this amazing man! Joyce questioned local teachers and librarians and found them in agreement. James Oglethorpe, like George Washington, had come to be a remote "ancient" who peered down from stilted paintings and from a marble statue in the Georgia state Capitol rotunda—little more.

This was certainly not true with anyone who had shared the excitement of the archeological "digs" at Frederica. Certainly not true of any of the fortunate persons, from the Golden Isles or Washington, who worked with the energetic, courageous Margaret Davis Cate, under whose careful eye Fort Frederica National Monument was planned and brought to reality. Still, we found mostly vagueness, a kind of automatic reverence and respect, but little real interest in the man Oglethorpe among our hundreds of new friends and acquaintances in coastal Georgia. As I toured the country from the West Coast to the East last summer, I did some checking. People had heard of James Edward Oglethorpe, but that was about it.

Daily I watched Joyce's interest mount. I could see a new manuscript fever setting in! The look in the eye, the absent-minded conversation at mealtime. All the signs were there. We were going to get that book the librarians wanted and needed.

At the time, Joyce was putting the finishing touches on the typescript of another short, pungent biographical master-piece, *John Adams, Farmer from Braintree, Champion of Independence*. I felt certain she wouldn't have enough left after that arduous task to tackle Oglethorpe anytime soon. But we've long learned to leave each other alone when "a new book is aborning." I said little, and then one day she drove down our lane and around the corner to Fort Frederica to spend an entire day in the Margaret Davis Cate Memorial Library—a gold mine for anyone working in coastal history. When she came back up our lane that evening, the die was cast. She had been hooked by James Edward Oglethorpe and began at once, between more long sessions at the Cate Library and voluminous correspondence with Lilla Hawes in Savannah, Phinizy Spaulding at the University of Georgia, and other Oglethorpe authorities, to fool around with Chapter One.

In no time at all, for us, James Edward Oglethorpe had come down from the picture on the museum wall, had leaped down from that stiff marble pedestal on the Georgia state Capitol landing—had begun to live. I should say, we had begun to "live" with him.

We have "lived" with some pretty fascinating people since we built our home in the woods near where Oglethorpe built the town of Frederica so long ago: Martha Berry, Sir Wilfred Grenfell, Theodore Roosevelt, John Adams, Horace Bunch Gould, Anson Dodge—but our "Oglethorpe period" is one I know I will never forget. And one of the big reasons I will never forget the weeks and months during which I watched Joyce's stack of manuscript grow is the poignant, little-known contact between John Adams, the gentleman from Braintree, and James Oglethorpe as a very old man. Joyce's *John Adams* came out in the early summer, and it seems more than coincidence that her new Oglethorpe biography is the very next book to be published.

Near the end of James Oglethorpe's long and exciting life, when he was eighty-nine years old, he walked alone to the rooms of the first, somewhat frightened and harassed American ambassador to Britain to have a talk about which few people know. The gentleman in the uncomfortable position of being ambassador to the country from which we had just wrested our freedom was John Adams. He must have trembled a little when ancient but still energetic General Oglethorpe entered his rooms that day. I can imagine Adams

72

wondering "What next?" He had not been treated warmly, needless to say, in London at that point in history. But James Edward Oglethorpe made him welcome! The king had tried, but understandably the press and the people still held their grudges against the impudent new country across the water.

Even after many readings of the manuscript, I still cannot avoid a slightly misty eye when I read the last pages of Joyce's new book. James Edward Oglethorpe had loved America— Georgia in particular—with the great passion of his long, adventurous life. He had come to assure the young ambassador that he understood what Americans were all about. That he, a British subject, was *with us*. That he understood why we had fought for the freedom to be ourselves.

Since the publication of *John Adams* and *James Edward Oglethorpe*, I have read both books again. As a result, I am not only freshly aware of the humanity of both men, I am able to read today's newspapers and listen to today's newscasts with a great deal more objectivity and calm.

I have come to believe that our one big lack as we begin what could be the Sick Seventies is a true, objective, historical perspective. You've heard this before. So have I. Why don't we make some effort to achieve a realistic view of what our country has achieved and where it has gone wrong during these almost two hundred years? Are we too busy fuming about all we see wrong now? Are we too conditioned to believe America is God's pampered cosmic pet? Are we too radical to the Right or to the Left to see straight ahead anymore? We are all of these things, I believe, and I am sorry for us. Sorry for us and ashamed of us. Both John Adams and James Oglethorpe were bridge-layers, not barrier-builders. One followed the other in the succession of our country's history, but each man, faulty as he was, kept to a realistic, sane purpose. John Adams' cousin Sam was a radical who probably thought John a square. James Oglethorpe put his own fortune, even his life, on the line for the sake of the underprivileged, and he had to contend constantly with the British Establishment, some of whom thought him extreme, too liberal. The labels continue to be stuck on, prejudice still is nurtured by extremists on both sides, but a look at the facts about the lives of Adams and Oglethorpe can be an enormously freeing experience.

Our decade is neither the worst nor the best of times. Our history has been bloody from its beginning. Our ideals are no more on trial now than before. If we see this clearly, objectively, with cool heads and warm hearts, we can hope for ourselves and our world, because seeing is the first step toward doing.

# CHAPTER XIV

# Love Came Down

Love came down to earth at Christmas—the first Christmas. Love also came down to St. Simons Island early in December, 1970. Love lives here!

After a long, back-tiring day of rewrite on the manuscript of *Lighthouse*, the third and last in the St. Simons trilogy, Joyce and I enjoyed a quiet, beautifully prepared dinner and good conversation with our beloved friends, Mr. and Mrs. George Barry of Sea Island. George Barry, I am eternally proud to say, built my house in the woods at Frederica. Of course, because it is mine and because he built it, it is to me the world's most comfortable, most beautiful, and dearest house.

We left the Barry's home fairly early—I am an early riser when deadlines approach—and as always, when we drove up our winding lane, we both were looking forward to opening the door of the dear house. I have yet to walk into it that I haven't appreciated the simple beauty of its old-fashioned lines. I have yet to walk into my house without being glad that it belongs both to the American National Bank and to me. Last night was no exception. Coming home should quiet all our hearts, calm our spirits, cause us to feel safe. Coming home always does that for me.

Since her recent surgery, Joyce has been living in the guest room downstairs, and so we stopped off there to read the *Brunswick News* and the Atlanta papers before going to bed. Joyce had just squeezed toothpaste onto the brush when I called in: "Do you smell something hot?" She did and so did I, and the smell got hotter and hotter and we looked at each other and thought about how far we were from a fire hydrant and how far from the St. Simons fire station itself.

We had just had a man up to rejuvenate our many fire extinguishers, but there wasn't any fire to extinguish—not that we could see. Just that hot and hotter smell. Strong, acrid, like an electric heater turned on for the first time since last winter. It was centered, this terrifying smell, in the guest room and the flower room that connects the guest room and the garage to the main house.

One of us tried to turn on the guest-room thermostat. At first it wouldn't come on, then it did. We decided to turn it off, just in case. We looked at each other again and one of us said, "Better call Gerald Buchan." Gerald installed our furnace and air conditioning system, and besides, he comes at any hour and he can fix anything. The other one said, "Better call the fire department, too!"

In the middle of this, the telephone rang. It was Phyllis Barry telling us we had forgotten something at their house, and without thinking how it would alarm her, I blurted, "Thanks so much for calling and for a beautiful evening, but I've got to call the fire department and Gerald Buchan!"

Then all the love I mentioned began arriving. Within eleven minutes after I called, in came a fire truck and the Sea Island security officer—and Gerald Buchan. Riding along

76

with gentlemanly Mr. Carl O. Svendsen from the St. Simons Fire Department was Mr. George Stevens, Jr., a descendant of Captain Charles Stevens, one of my favorite characters in my novel, *New Moon Rising*. No two middle-aged, somewhat frightened gals could have had lovelier, more considerate 11 P.M. callers! With Gerald, the men from the firehouse felt walls, checked sockets, lamps, extension cords, and sniffed right along with us.

Somehow I found myself out in the front yard making sure my cherished, silvered, cedar-shingle roof was intact, and there stood the kind officer from Sea Island, keeping a string of cars bearing the curious off my newly planted rye grass. He didn't act the way "tough cops" are supposed to act at all. He was reassuring, sympathetic—as though he really cared whether my house was going to catch fire or not. I could have cried with gratitude.

Inside, Joyce and the fireman and Gerald Buchan were still searching attics and all rooms, and then I remembered the Barrys and how worried they must be about us and our house. When I called them there was no answer. The helpful Sea Island operator tried several times with loving patience. Operators at hotel switchboards just don't do this, but ours do. "The Barrys are on their way over here," Joyce guessed, and I knew she was right. The Barrys bless our lives by loving us. Sure enough, the next set of lights to turn in at my gate belonged to the Barry's car. Gerald was in the attic of the guest house by then, doing all the skillful and mysterious things Gerald Buchan can do with wirings and appliances. Just as George Barry's welcome face appeared at our back door, good news came from the attic that Gerald had found the trouble!

Something having to do with a "sealed something or other" of a fan that does something equally mysterious—in order to keep us cool in summer and warm in winter—had burned out.

We couldn't get a new one until Monday, but that was all right. Joyce had been meaning to move back upstairs to her own rooms anyway. We whooped with joy, hugged Gerald and George Barry, and the telephone rang again.

This time it was the Sea Island operator, still concerned about us, telling me she had recognized my voice the last time I tried to call the Barrys and that Mr. George Barry wanted me to call Mr. Buddy Culver. Now the Thurberesque sequence was beginning. Not knowing that I had called Gerald Buchan, who worked for Buddy Culver when my marvelous heating and cooling system had been installed, George Barry had called for Buddy. Buddy was to call me during the minutes it took the Barrys to drive from Sea Island to my place, but Buddy didn't have my number and it is unlisted. So Buddy had been calling the Brunswick operator, who had been trying to reach me for a full half hour. . . . She couldn't get me because I was madly trying to dial Buddy Culver to tell him we were going to be all right.

Satisfied that disconnecting the faulty fan would remove all danger of a fire, our loving helpers began to roll away around our narrow, winding shell road. First the nice policeman, then the red fire truck, then Gerald, and last of all, our faithful hosts of what seemed by now a long time ago, the George Barrys.

The last person out the gate, Mr. Barry or Gerald Buchan, locked it and we turned out our big flood lights, looked at each other again and said: "We're all right. It wasn't anything Gerald can't fix. Our house is all right. There wasn't a fire. And we're so blessed to live on this Island where people love each other, we've got to find a way to let them know."

Tired, relieved, we loaded our arms with Joyce's reading lamp, heating pad, pile of books, and pillows, and headed upstairs. I had just dumped the pillows on her bed on the second floor when the telephone rang again. "Miss Price?" The voice was so concerned. "This is the Brunswick operator. Is everything all right? Did you ever get in touch with Mr. Culver?"

Well, you won't believe this if you're visiting our Island from the North, but I just broke down and told her the whole story? And—*she listened*. And she was interested and relieved and glad and happy and thankful that the problem had been solved. Over an hour had passed and this thoughtful operator was still trying to help. I told her I loved her and thanked her for all the fine service we get from Southern Bell. We hung up, finally, but both Joyce and I were bowled over by the fact that a telephone operator cared about *us*.

We got ready for bed, scanned the papers—kept going over the excitement of the evening. Joyce said: "Well, it's just more proof that Love did come down that first Christmas." I agreed. We said goodnight and I went to my room to open my mail which had been put aside that day. In the stack of letters was a dull-looking green statement from my bank. Joyce and I have a small joint savings account in case of emergency, and the green slip told us that we had made a little interest this year. With the green slip was a small white form explaining something about audits. I "read at" it, but my attention was caught by the word "over" written in red ink at the bottom. I turned the printed form over and found these words written by hand:

"MERRY CHRISTMAS TO YOU BOTH FROM SOME MORE OF YOUR FANS AND FRIENDS AT AMERICAN NATIONAL!"

That was the final straw. I felt tears sting my eyes. What could have been a harassing, exhausting evening had turned into a love feast. Love did come down that first Christmas, and He is still here moving toward us in love; always toward us—never away.

# CHAPTER XV

# *Journey to Reality*

The slogan "Putting Christ Back in Christmas" has always seemed utterly ridiculous to me. It is impossible to take Him out of Christmas! I realize the slogan implies that we have seemingly forgotten that Christmas is the celebration of the birth of Christ, as we "deck our halls" and streets and stores and homes with tinsel and styrofoam balls glittering with pinned-on sequins. But the slogan has always left me with an empty feeling.

Far more important, in my opinion—certainly more positive—would be to set aside a little time in the midst of the package-wrapping and shopping and tree-trimming (fun as it all is) to think about the One whose birthday we celebrate. We will read the Gospel accounts of His coming; our church choirs will sing carols and cantatas proclaiming the Holy Night—the Advent of our Lord. But there is more we should do if we really want to *experience* Christmas.

We, ourselves, one by on, should take time—late at night, early some morning—simply to think about what really happened that first Christmas day almost two thousand years ago.

Christmas trees are fine—I put mine up almost as soon as

they go on sale at the Kiwanis Club lot in Brunswick. Joyce and I spend two fun-filled days decorating our tree. Before we left on our last autographing tour of the year early in December, we managed to litter the house with packing cartons and bright paper and ribbons as we began our own gift-wrapping. My mother comes each year to St. Simons Island to spend Christmas with me, and for two whole weeks I stop all writing, answer almost no letters. I "play" Christmas to the hilt. I'm all for it.

But twenty Christmases ago I experienced my first Christmas of knowing the reason behind it all. I had blithely sung carols about "God and sinners reconciled" all my life without having the foggiest notion of what the line actually meant. Then twenty years ago, I was reconciled to Him and I knew. For the first time in my life, I realized that God was discoverable to anyone—not just to men trained in seminaries or women devoted to the cloistered life. God, I found, was discoverable to me. Every day of every year since that first shining discovery, I have learned something new, something more about what He is really like.

In my thinking, this is the one key to adequate living: the continuing discovery of what God is really like. If we know someone, we know whether or not he or she can be trusted.

Faith comes as an almost automatic by-product of knowing God *as He is*. And there is, to my knowledge, no other way to find out about Him except in Jesus Christ. My theology is simple: God saw that man was not catching on to His real nature, and so He came to earth in the Person of Jesus of Nazareth. It is one thing to discuss principles of theology, but when our hearts are broken, we cannot be satisfied with a principle. Just as a troubled child wants not the mother principle but Mother, in person, so we need God to be a discoverable Person.

He is—in Jesus Christ. He came as a man, not so that He

81

would understand how it feels to be human, but so that *we* would know that He knows. All that could be contained of God in a human being came that Holy Night in the stable at Bethlehem, and so that no one could ever say he was not good enough to be a Christian, God picked out the lowliest possible circumstances in which to be born: to humble, hard-working parents from the hill country of Nazareth, God Himself chose to be born into human history on a pile of straw, with only the heat from the bodies of animals in the stable around Him for comfort.

Christmas is not merely a beautiful thought. Christmas is the beginning of man's continuing discovery of the true character of God. Christmas should be full of surprises for children—old and young—because God thought up the most magnificent surprise of all for us that night. But because now God is knowable even to the least among us, life no longer needs to surprise us with its blows and heartaches. No one who really knows God in Jesus Christ expects all of life to "come up roses." We don't expect this because Jesus said it wouldn't. The continuing discovery of what God is really like insulates us and gives us courage and humor and inner strength for living adequately in the midst of whatever life hands us. Whatever we have to face, Jesus, because of that first Christmas, has been there before us.

Christmas is all the fun and singing and laughter and surprises, but it began the journey to reality for man. Before Jesus came that deep, holy night, only the prophets and the scholars spoke of knowing God. Now, you and I can know Him, and can go on finding out more and more about Him, because He bothered to become one of us, to get into the whole wonderful, dreadful, joyful, tearful mess with us.

As Sister Corita wrote: "He is and He is here! The signs are all around us!"

Love did come down.

# CHAPTER XVI

# Only Customs Have Changed

I am living these days in a swinging, often confusing arc of chaos. My pendulum swings from the year 1792, a year in which trouble and intrigues were everywhere in the world, to this year of 1972, where trouble and intrigues are also everywhere in our world.

Yes, I'm at work on another historical novel, *Don Juan McQueen*, and not having a very easy time of it. For seven months I've spent my days in the complex history of the Georgia-Florida border, in the struggles of our then-new nation, the repercussions still resounding from our own Revolution, and the bitterness and bloodshed and inhumanity of the French Revolution. Travel and communications in those days were slow, but each part of a warring world affected each other part, as now. There were no electronic devices for "bugging" opponent's political headquarters, but man's tricky nature managed to spy just the same.

If I sound cynical, sorry about that. I'm not really. I'm just passing through one of those times we should all have to experience: an open-eyed look at the facts of human nature. Man has always been both lovable and despicable; both honorable and filled with deception. Populations have always been both prosperous and poor; both ill and healthy. Man's heart has always been capable of love and hate; of bitterness and joy; of grief and high spirits. Our society has always had mansions and hovels. Children have always been born with retarded minds and with bright minds. The elderly, staying with us longer these days, are still, as always, both lonely and cared for; both wanted and unwanted.

We have not come far and we have come very far. The paradox invites examination.

It so happens that I'm working this year in the social context which extended from Charleston, South Carolina, down into Savannah and around the coast into what was then Spanish East Florida. Most of the United States was coastal, and in both Charleston and Savannah, there was wealth— mansions far superior to ours now, handsome buildings for the conduct of business, churches with architecture to inspire worship. But there was also poverty. Black poverty and white poverty.

In St. Augustine, the seat of government during both the First and Second Spanish periods, life was a struggle. True, during the twenty years in which England ruled Florida, there was prosperity, especially after loyal American colonists began to pour over the Georgia border into the one British colony to remain faithful to the Crown of England. But in the time of my novel (the Second Spanish period), for breakfast at the tiny Spanish military hospital (restored now) wounded and fever-ridden patients were served lard soup and half a slice of dry bread! Even the average St. Augustine citizen ate according to the tides. Except for the ocean, the people of the city would have starved. The few stringy chickens ate so many crabs that stewed chicken tasted like fish.

There was no hospital at all for local citizens. There was only one doctor, whose first responsibility was to the military hospital. Retarded children were locked in rooms, and the elderly lay on pallets in the heat and flies. The soldiers, poorly trained and poorly clothed (in spite of the proud history of the Hibernian Regiment), were merely tossed into a stone-walled cell of the Castillo de San Marco when they grew lonely during their off-hours and drank too much. There wasn't a church building until the late 1790s and even that was called a "miracle of God" because money was so scarce; once the building was finished, no social services were available through its offices.

Sound gruesome? It was and it wasn't. This was a way of life, and no one missed Social Security, Medicare, the Red Cross, the Salvation Army, boys' clubs, or the school for retarded children. The lonely, bored soldiers of the Third Battalion did not miss the service men's club because no one had ever heard of such a thing.

Father Miquel O'Reilley and Father Hassett, the two caring, well-intentioned priests at St. Augustine, did all they could to remind the people of their sins, to encourage them in their spiritual pursuits. For the largely Minorcan population, there had been, until 1790, saintly Father Pedro Camps. But Father Camps died, exhausted by loving his people through the long years of hunger and agony, at the ill-fated New Smyrna Colony sixty miles down the coast from Augustine. People then existed on less than we can conceive, but they also loved and laughed and sang and played guitars and grew flowers and enjoyed oranges and grieved and hated and showed kindness and venom.

85

We still love and hate and grieve and enjoy. We still live and die; and when it isn't too much trouble, we show kindness, caring, and concern for our fellow-man. Have we improved? In some ways, yes. Those of us who grieve at the hacking away of the remainder of our earth's natural beauty often think that we long for the old days when virgin forests were in such abundance man didn't have to be careful. We like to read and to write books about the past when men and women took time to write letters, to visit one another, to make things by hand. Still, there has to be a balance somewhere: a balance, I mean, in our viewpoints. Human nature hasn't changed at all, so far as I can see.

In one way, I write my "novel people" as though they lived today. Customs are different. I can spend a whole afternoon trying to understand how a man once built a house or ran a water-powered sawmill. But men's hearts and spiritual needs have not changed.

Brown Pelican/St. Simons Marsh

# CHAPTER XVII

# We Are Blessed

As I write this early on a June day, the only thought that haunts my mind is that I have to leave St. Simons Island again in three days. For almost a month, I have been traveling, first to New York City, then to the West Coast, north to Portland, Oregon, and east to Denver, telling large audiences in person and on radio and TV that there is no place on earth like coastal Georgia. I am physically exhausted, far too weary to begin again to travel the East Coast and the Midwest for another month, but inside there is a slow, certain "filling in" taking place. If only I had just two more days here. I don't, though, and so I am having a rare opportunity to find out if there really is something therapeutic about our area. There is.

If I could have made it through the plane window, I fully believe the first glimpse of the marshes and the twisting salt creeks would have made it possible for me to have flown straight to St. Simons on my own eagerness to be back. How could one small strip of sandy land have become so surely my home after having lived most of my life in other places? I don't know the answer. I only know it has.

I'm sure part of the reason is the beauty—the tall pines, the welcoming living-room window, the brightly painted buntings, the towhees, the special yellow-throated warbler who waited for me to come back. I'm certain also that having found the warm, engrossing, encouraging story of the Gould family, around which I have built a trilogy of novels, is one of the central reasons St. Simons is my home. And it has been enlightening, heart-warming, strengthening to find people thousands of miles away from the Deep South and coastal Georgia as carried away with romance and wonder of our area as I am. I feel I have been able to build some bridges of understanding North to South on this trip.

As before the Civil War, Americans still need to come to know each other not as regions but as people. Everywhere I have gone, I have poured my energies into each TV show, each radio program, each press interview and speaking date, attempting to remind Americans that *we are one people*. That Southerners are *not* any more peculiar than Northerners.

I am almost too weary at this point to realize it, but when I can find a free minute to think back over the past weeks, I am amazed at the genuine interest people of all kinds, of all political and religious persuasions, have shown in the St. Simons trilogy. Almost without exception, they came up to me at the table where I was autographing at the close of a speaking date to say, "I've got to visit St. Simons Island: Your novels have made me fall in love with it, too. What is there about it that causes this?"

Whatever there is, it is not easy to put into words. I know I have felt like a fish out of water every minute I was gone. I will feel that way until I'm back to stay in July. Over the past

89

weeks I have seen the bright blue-and-pink ice plant cascading over rocky cliffs onto the white, white sand of the Pacific; I have experienced again the indescribable silence of the redwoods; I have seen the noble white crowns of Ranier and Hood; I have driven through the fragrant foothills of the Rocky Mountains outside Denver. It is all breathtaking, worth traveling the necessary miles to enjoy, but to me, at least, it could never be home now.

I am forever grateful to you who are my neighbors in coastal Georgia for your enthusiasm and response to my books about our beloved land, grateful to my friends the booksellers, grateful for the way you have accepted Joyce and me as "natives." But, today, in my extreme weariness and my sadness at having to leave again, I think I am most grateful that you are the kind of people you are. What can we do to stay natural, open-hearted, unashamed of real values and a genuine faith in God? Maybe the best thing we can do is to look a little longer at the next live oak we pass, at our marshes, remember to look up at night for a lingering minute more at our sky—still clear and spattered with honest stars, uncontaminated by smog and man-made pollution.

I was in many metropolitan areas for weeks, and often I didn't see the sun until 11:30 each morning. And never one sunset.

Well. I do have to leave now, but only for a time. And—I can come back. For those of us who live on St. Simons or merely visit, there is nothing further to say beyond this: "We are blessed. We are blessed."